"Ninety percent of all millionaires become so through owning real estate. More money has been made in real estate than in all industrial investments combined. The wise young man or wage earner of today invests his money in real estate."

—Andrew Carnegie

READ THIS FIRST

Just to say thanks for getting this book, I would like to give you the Audiobook version *100% FREE!*

TO DOWNLOAD FOR FREE GO TO:
HaydenCrabtree.com/freebook

FOREWORD

Subscribe to my YouTube channel

For Weekly Real Estate Investing Content

Go to YouTube and search
"Hayden Crabtree"

**Subscribe to Hayden's
YouTube channel**

W e've all seen the house-flipping shows on TV. They take the ugliest junker house on the block that are full of problems, and within a 20 minute time frame they turn them into world class homes!

We are in awe..

It looks so fun. It looks so easy.

Excited and inspired after binge-watching an entire season in a day, you decide "I'm going to start investing in real estate! Let's go flip a house!"

So you go junker house shopping. After seeing 10 overpriced houses, you get tired of looking and pull the trigger on one. You pay too much... but they *always* pay too much on TV and still come out ahead on the deal.

After you buy the house, you start swinging a hammer. Day after day. Week after week. When you realize you're in over your head, you decide to call a contractor to get some professional help. When they come out, you are told you have several permit violations, and the remaining work is going to be double what you originally thought it would be.

Your highly profitable and fun house flip just turned into a money pit nightmare.

"Maybe Real Estate isn't for me" you think to yourself as you calculate how much money you are going to lose on this house.

This is the sad story of most people's first interaction with trying to make money in real estate. They don't realize that house flipping isn't *real* investing.

Building wealth in real estate is not about making money quickly and repeating again and again.

Building wealth in real estate is about creating an asset that yields residual income forever, reduces your taxes, letting other people pay off your debts for you, and patiently waiting for your investment value to rise.

It's not just house flippers that have it wrong. Everyone who has put their blind fold on and hands their hard earned money over to wall street is just as naive.

The saddest part of this whole story is that building wealth in real estate is actually very easy when you have the right information and are willing to take control of your money.

That's exactly what *Skip The Flip* is all about.

Not only does this book show the exact strategies that the wealthiest investors in the world are using, it also breaks it down into an easy to understand, step-by-step playbook that anyone can follow.

Where most books focus on one single piece of the real estate puzzle, this book hits all the points that professional real estate investors use to grow their wealth and cash flow.

The good news for you is that you don't have to take the slow track like so many investors do at the start of their venture. Everything you need to know about the real estate industry is wrapped up in a single package here.

Hayden's approach to real estate investing is exactly what I am doing today, and exactly what I would do if I were starting from 0. The strategies he uses are world class, tried and true wealth building principles that elite investors use.

If you want to learn how the wealthy think about real estate investing, this book is for you.

- Ken McElroy
  - Best Selling Author
  - Owner of MC Companies
  - $750 Million Portfolio
  - Rich Dad Advisor

PREFACE

Contrary to what most people believe, I think you should share your business "secrets". I like to practice an abundance mindset, which to me means that there is plenty of success on this earth to be had by both you and me. If I let you in on how to make money in real estate, that is not going to keep me from making money in real estate, so I should be generous and teach you everything I know.

This book contains the information you need to skip house flipping and move directly into investing for long term wealth and monthly cash flow.

Flipping houses will make you money. Investing in cash flow real estate will make you wealthy.

This book is written to be informative, but more importantly useful.

You are going to learn everything useful I know about finance and real estate from my college degree and also what I have learned in my real world experience. I hope you take this advice and apply it in your own life, as I am writing this book as a tool that I would have given myself to read at the beginning of my own journey.

CONTENTS

INTRODUCTION

So how did this book come about? I was at a conference and I left inspired and confused at the same time. I scratched my head in disbelief as I walked out of the hotel. "How could they not all be aware of what a huge opportunity exists?" I asked my friend and fellow real estate investor, Hunter. To me it seemed like it was such common knowledge. Such a simple path that *anyone* can capitalize on to build extreme wealth, reduce their taxes and generate monthly cash flow.

The event I am speaking about is when I reconnected with 35 high level entrepreneurs and business minded people at a reunion. It was an incredible weekend because so many smart people were in the room. We had people with their own businesses, and others that were tearing through the ranks at some of the biggest companies in America.

As I talked to each individual about what they were up to these days, I got such cool and awesome stories about how they are changing the world with big data or revolutionizing different industries. As they reciprocated the question, "What are you doing these days?" I would have to catch myself and say, "Real estate investing" which is typically my short answer. If I'm not careful I can talk about real estate for hours without taking a breath.

Like you, lots of people have an interest in real estate investing. After talking with many people, I have learned that real estate investing has many different meanings to each individual.

Also like you, many smart people at very high levels are not aware of some of the largest "behind the scenes" benefits of real estate. These benefits are so huge that they can change his or her financial life drastically.

You should take a different approach than most when considering getting into their first real estate investment. The way many people get into investing is the S L O W track, and there is a much faster way for you to get started in real estate.

You should *Skip the Flip*...

As I dive in to exactly what it is I do, I can start to see the eyes of the other person light up, almost in disbelief. "That makes so much sense! Can I take you out to lunch sometime and pick your brain some more?"

The reason for this book is because the majority of Americans live paycheck to paycheck, don't have a reliable secondary income stream, and know very little about how true wealth is built in the modern world we live in. The truth of what used to be "get a job with a good company, invest in a 401k and get a pension", is long gone. Younger generations will not have pensions or social security to rely on. We are going to have to fend for ourselves on this economic planet. I tell them, "It doesn't matter if you have $5,000,000, $5,000 or $5, there is a way for you to get started building wealth in the most durable and recession resistant asset in the world: Cash Flow Real Estate."

In this book, you are going to learn how cash flow real estate is less risky and more profitable than any other investment. You are also going to learn a simple and proven system you can use to grow your wealth and monthly cash flow exponentially, no matter how much cash you have right now.

I graduated college at the top of my class with a real estate and finance degree. But, before I graduated at 22 years old, I had flipped several houses, owned 6 residential rental properties, was a partner in 2 commercial properties and had helped others buy more than $7 Million of investment properties.

After reading this book, you will be able to use tools to shield your income and decrease your tax bill, value any piece of investment real estate in under 60 seconds, know the difference between good debt and bad debt. This will help you assemble an action plan to grow your wealth in real estate investing *the right way.*

Robert Kiyosaki of *Rich Dad, Poor Dad* teaches us the rich do not work for money. The rich use money to buy assets that make them more money. The average millionaire has 7 streams of income, and you are going to learn in this book how to get started building reliable and massive streams of income from real estate, each and every month.

After reading this book, I promise you will fully understand how to profit from real estate and build multiple streams of income. AND I promise you will learn everything I learned from my college real estate degree (and more) in under 200 pages. This book is designed to be a short and sweet guide. It will not waste any of your precious time on information you don't need to know. Every page is going to be useful and applicable.

Don't be the person who misses out on life changing deals that they see everyday, without even realizing it, because they refused to invest in their financial education. Be the kind of person who takes responsibility for his or her financial life. Be the kind of person who creates wealth for themselves and their family that will last forever.

The information in the following pages is solely responsible for CREATING 90% of the world's millionaires. If you know what you are doing in real estate you can earn millions in residual income each year. But, if you do not educate yourself on the fundamentals and the right systems, you can lose it all like many did in 2008. This book is the operating system for your brain that will allow you to see opportunities that will create life changing wealth for yourself and those around you.

ARE YOU READY?! … OK! LET'S GO!!

DEBUNK MYTHS

Before we get started with the fundamentals of successful real estate investing, let's do a mindset check. The most important thing you can do to fast-track to success is to adopt a new mindset.

If you are stuck with an old mindset, the information you read will not resonate and will not impact your actions. That is not what we want, as information is only good if you put it to work.

The information in the following chapters has cost me more than $50,000 in college education, and $20,000+ in seminar and coaching fees. It has also taken years of my life to discover much of this information through trial and error. You are going to be able to take full advantage of that by reading these pages.

To start working on your new mindset, let's debunk some myths you have heard that aren't true and will hold you back from real estate success.

CHAPTER 1

REAL ESTATE LICENSE

You do not need a real estate degree or license to make money in real estate. Many people think that to get involved in real estate investing they need to go through the process of testing and getting licensed to become an agent or a broker. In fact, the opposite is true. Getting your real estate license can actually hinder you from making better investments. When you have your real estate license, you are held to certain standards that will present friction to your investing success.

The most successful investor I know does not have a license, and you do not need one either to get started!

We are going to talk in this book about what an investor does and how they make money. You do not need a license to be a great investor, so do not let this idea slow you down!

CHAPTER 2

DEBT IS BAD

You have heard about people who want to change their financial life and as a kickstart they cut up their credit cards. This is not your path to wealth. You must get comfortable with debt to shortcut your success in real estate investing.

We will dive deep into debt in Section 8, but for now, you need to understand that debt is neither good nor bad. Instead, debt is a tool. It is what the user makes it. Debt is good AND debt is bad.

Think of debt as a chainsaw. When used correctly, a chainsaw can help you cut down trees in a tenth of the time it would take without a chainsaw. With an axe it may take you an hour to cut down a tree. With a chainsaw, you can do it in less than 10 minutes. While that chainsaw is very useful, if it is not treated with care and respect, it can cause a lot of harm.

Do not listen to anyone who says "all debt is bad", as that person is unaware of the potential benefits debt can have. If you look at the USA, we have a massive debt. While some think that is bad, that same debt that has helped expand our economy to a global powerhouse and has given our people one of the highest standards of living in the world.

At the time of writing this book, Apple has $245 billion in cash, but they still choose to use debt. Why is that? They know that when debt is used correctly, it can have a positive outcome on their profits.

CHAPTER 3

YOU DON'T NEED MONEY

"I don't have any money to invest in real estate."

This is one of the biggest mental blocks that prevents so many people from getting started investing. There are several strategies you can use to overcome this road block, and you are going to learn a few ways in this book.

When I first got started in real estate, this was my strongest limiting belief. I thought I would never become a real estate success until I had piles of my own money I could use. It wasn't until I hired a coach and learned skills to see that having money is not a real reason to not invest in real estate and start building wealth.

One great example of how to overcome this is found in the bonus section of this book and shows you how I "bought" a $3,000,000 property that profits $108,000 a year with *no money of my own.*

Yes... you read that right. $108,000 a year with no money. You can do the same!

The first key to getting over this mental block is learning all about how investing works and building confidence in yourself as an investor. That comes with education and is a process everyone must go through. You are on the right road to educating yourself by reading this book.

CHAPTER 4

REAL ESTATE RISK

If you listen to many people who got crushed in 2008, they will tell you to stay out of real estate. What many do not know about the crash of 2008 is that some investors became extremely wealthy during that time. They built massive wealth because they capitalized on the mistakes of others. You can too if you understand the fundamental laws of investing!

The investors who lost during 2008 were not following the fundamental laws of real estate investing outlined in this book. The investors who used good fundamentals, like the ones taught here, are the people who created life changing wealth.

The main fundamental to follow to avoid pain in a recession is to *buy real estate for cash flow* rather than to flip it for a one time profit.

While all investing carries some risk, if you follow the fundamental laws you can drastically reduce the risk and set yourself up to make it through (and profit from) any downturn or recession.

CHAPTER 5

HOUSE FLIPPING (OR WHOLESALING) IS INVESTING

Flipping houses can produce a tremendous income for people who do it successfully. But flipping houses is not investing, and it is not how wealth is created in real estate. By flipping houses rather than investing, you spin your wheels always looking to buy and sell. You will have a hard time creating the stability and cash flow that is produced from commercial real estate investing.

Flipping houses is an active job, or it is a business you can create. Do not confuse yourself by thinking flipping houses is investing. Flipping is not bad if you are looking for a job or a side hustle to create some extra income. The goal of flipping houses should be to create extra money to put into cash flow real estate that is going to pay you each month for the rest of your life.

For those who have heard of (or currently are) wholesaling, know that wholesaling is not investing in real estate, like flipping houses is not investing. Wholesaling is a business that involves connecting a buyer and a seller for a fee.

For those who do not know what wholesaling is, we will get into that briefly in chapter 14.

Also, flipping and wholesaling do not provide many of the tremendous behind the scenes benefits that real investing does. You will learn all about these benefits through these pages.

I actually prefer wholesaling to flipping because wholesaling is like flipping, but takes out a lot of your risk.

CHAPTER 6

YOUR HOME IS NOT AN INVESTMENT

To understand why this is a myth, let's quickly define what an asset is and what a liability is.

An asset is something that puts money into your pocket.

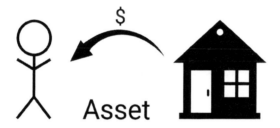

A liability is something that takes money out of your pocket.

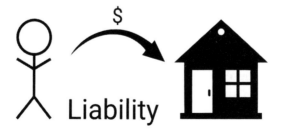

Your goal in real estate investing is to acquire assets that pay you money every month, without having to do any work. Meaning you would still get paid if you are on vacation, or if you are doing other work that you love.

When you acquire assets that pay you more than the money you spend, you have *financial freedom*. You can rely on your assets to pay for your expenses rather than relying on a job. Financial freedom is the ultimate goal!

Back to why your house you live in is not a good investment.

Homes that are purchased for personal use cost money. You have to pay for repairs, insurance, taxes and mortgage payments. All this is money that is coming out of your pocket. This is the definition of a liability.

On the flip side, if that home is rented out and starts to produce income that went into your pocket, it could become an asset if it were cash flow positive.

The idea that a home is a great investment is sold to us by the big banks who need customers for loans. The banks make money when someone borrows money from them. To increase their profits, they need to make more loans. So they sell the idea of the "American dream" as owning your own home with a white picket fence around the front yard. When you finally achieve the "American dream" of home ownership you go borrow money from them to buy the home and they make more money.

I am not against home ownership, but you need to understand that a home you live in is a liability and not an asset.

Many of you reading this right now saying, " but a home value will increase and I will make a return on it that way." That is true, but the fundamental law of real estate investing for wealth is invest for cash flow. A house you live in does not pay you, so it is not an asset. If we bet on appreciation *we are gambling, not investing.*

Now that I have addressed some of these flawed mindsets, you can set those aside and focus on the upcoming lessons. Use this chapter as a reference when you hear these myths come up on your real estate investing journey.

If you have any questions about any of these myths, visit my website at haydencrabtree.com/resources and submit your question. I will get back to you to help clarify.

RE VS STOCKS

The next step in your journey is to comprehend the difference in real estate vs other forms of investing. When most people think about investing they think about the stock market. I think the stock market is a roller coaster that I do not want to ride. Real estate is fundamentally different than the stock market.

Before I got started on my real estate journey, I looked at stock investing. I would study books about the fundamentals of stocks, research companies, and look at technical analysis. It got very old, very quickly. I dreaded staring at charts all day, hoping that the price would go up or down in my favor. I did not have any control on the market price of the stocks I wanted to buy or sell.

I want to be able to *control my investment!* This is where real estate is different than the stock market.

You do not control stocks.

You do control real estate.

Many people counter this argument citing that Warren Buffet, the greatest investor of all time, made his fortune in stocks. While he has had great success investing in stocks, I always point out that Warren Buffet is not only buying stocks. Warren Buffet is buying businesses. Warren buys such large chunks of companies so that he can control them strategically and add value to them over long periods of time. I don't know about you, but I do not want to wait 10+ years to see the fruits of my labor… and I want more control in my monthly cash flow.

Let's talk through a few points to illustrate how the life of a real estate investor is different than that of a stock investor.

CHAPTER 7

CONTROL

Real estate gives its owner the ability to control the value of his or her assets. You cannot control the value of your stocks no matter how hard you try.

You can spend endless hours researching stocks, but you still cannot control the value of the investment. With stock investing, the fate of your money is in the hands of someone else and you are subject to being manipulated.

In real estate investing, you control the value of your asset. You do not wake up one morning to see that a tweet from the President has made the value of your money increase or decrease 10%. One of the biggest lessons to take away from this book is that real estate is superior to all other forms of investing due to the level of control the owner has.

Put yourself in a position to control your destiny! Do not rely on other people to do this for you!

CHAPTER 8

TANGIBLE

Real estate is… well, real. You can touch it. You can use it. You can visit it, improve it, make alterations. The great thing about real estate investing is you own a piece of the world. It's one of a kind, nothing else like it in the world.

If you own a share of Apple stock, you own only one of 800 million identical shares. The piece that you have cannot be touched, it cannot be altered by you, and you can't walk into Apple and say "let's change this up over here. I think we could make more money if we did it this way." You are on their fictitious roller coaster.

If you own a short term rental property on the beach, you can vacation there.

If you own an apartment complex, you can live there.

If you own a storage facility, you can store your things there.

How can you use a stock if you own it? It is not real, it is not tangible.

CHAPTER 9

PREDICTABLE

In the stock market, the general value tends to rise as time moves forward. But you cannot predict what your stocks will be worth tomorrow, next month or next year. Many have a large majority of their wealth that they have worked their whole life for tied up in a few stocks. What happens when that company releases lower than expected earnings and the stocks value drops instantly?

Poof. Gone.

That wasn't a part of your financial plan, was it? The point here is that you should invest with as much certainty and predictability as possible.

Real estate is predictable. Before you buy it you can very accurately estimate how much money you are going to make and when. You know that rent is due on the first, and how much that rent is going to be. You know how much your property is worth, and how much you can get if you sell that property.

Don't let someone else control you. You control you!

CHAPTER 10

DEBT IS YOUR FRIEND

The definition of leverage is to use something to its maximum advantage.

That could be a crowbar to open a door. We are using a piece of metal to do something we cannot do on our own.

It could be hiring an attorney to handle legal matters for you. We are hiring an attorney who has knowledge we do not have to do something for us. We are leveraging that attorney for our benefit.

In the case of real estate, we use banks to help us buy more real estate than we can afford with our own cash. You are likely already familiar with this concept through mortgage lending.

When buying a house for $100,000 you can go to the bank and they will give you $80,000 and you have to put in $20,000 of your own money. This concept, leverage, allows us to buy more assets than we could buy on our own. We use other people's money to increase our personal wealth.

If you had $100,000 you could buy the house for $100,000 by yourself. Because we are able to use leverage and buy that same house for $20,000 of our own money and $80,000 of a banks money we can now buy 5 houses instead of one.

There is massive power in leverage in real estate!

Section 8 details leverage and the benefits it will bring to your life.

CHAPTER 11

POLITICAL RISK

L ove them or hate them, it doesn't matter. Politicians impact our entire economy. When the President tweets about foreign policy, interest rates, or anything else for that matter, he impacts the lives of everyone invested in the stock market.

Meanwhile, real estate investors know that their properties are going to keep producing cash, shielding their taxes, and building wealth. We real estate investors don't care, and barely notice what is happening on Wall Street and in the news. We keep collecting our rent checks on the first of every month, having our tenants pay for our expenses, our debt, and putting cash in our pocket each and every month.

CHAPTER 12

SHIELD YOUR INCOME

We are going to go through a whole section of tax benefits later, but for now you need to understand and be aware that there are loopholes and incentives in the U.S. tax code that allows real estate investors to write off "ghost expenses". These benefits do not come to house flippers, agents, brokers, or wholesalers. They only come to true investors.

We get to take large expenses that we didn't actually have to pay for and put them on our tax returns. These will shield our income from taxes, and allows us to make money without it being taxed in any way. It is very powerful and very real.

With the large tax benefits, it is possible for an investor to buy an entire property with the same money they were going to pay in taxes.

Do not ignore Section 7 on tax benefits. Taxes are most people's #1 largest expense. If you could eliminate your largest expense every year, how would your financial life change?

CHAPTER 13

GET CREATIVE

Real estate investing allows you to be creative! Trying to strike a deal to buy a property? Get creative!

There are endless options out there that you can use to meet your needs as an investor, and the needs of the owner of a property you would like to buy. You can also be creative with how you run a property to increase income, decrease expenses, make your tenants happier. This will increase the value of your property! You cannot do this in stocks because with stocks you are not in control.

Real estate = Control, stability, predictability, tax benefits

Stocks = No control, manipulation, taxes on profits

To recap, in real estate you have control, can use your property to benefit yourself, can predict your future income, use debt as your friend, use a bank's money to make yourself wealthy, enjoy tax benefits and use creativity to get a deal done.

Hopefully you're beginning to see why real estate is a more stable and productive place to put your financial future than the stock market.

Real estate investing is like playing offense in football. You are calling the plays, putting blockers in place so you can score and deciding which players to give the ball to.

Investing in stocks is like playing defense. You have to try and predict what the other team is going to do, and if you are wrong, well… you lose. It's being proactive vs being reactive. When it comes to your money, be proactive… be in control.

DIFFERENT WAYS TO MAKE MONEY IN REAL ESTATE

To give you a brief background on the specific angle you are going to learn for real estate investing, you need to have a quick overview of all the different ways one can make a profit in real estate. This way when you are talking to others you have a base level education and will sound like a professional. Read below to get a quick description of each path with the Pro's and Con's of each angle.

CHAPTER 14

WHAT IS WHOLESALING?

What is it? Wholesaling property is a great way to make money from real estate without actually buying it. A wholesaler can sometimes be referred to as a bird dog.

What a wholesaler does is go into the marketplace and look for deals that they can sell to an investor who wants to buy the property for long term investment. They may also be looking for a house that a house flipper would like to buy and flip.

The steps to performing a wholesale are as follows: the wholesaler drives around neighborhoods or goes online to find properties that meet what they are looking for. They get a list of all the properties that could be a fit. They then begin to contact the owners of those properties and ask them if they would like to sell the property. Most of the properties that they are looking for are in bad shape and need work. This is a sign of motivation that they may want to sell (good thing for a property buyer). While many of the owners tell them no, some will say they would like to sell.

At this point the wholesaler would like to gain control of this property. They can do that by putting the property "under contract." This is a formal agreement between the buyer and the seller that they have a deal, but the buyer needs some time before they can actually give the seller the money for the property (this is standard).

Once the property is under contract, if the contract is written correctly, the seller cannot make an agreement to sell the property to any other buyer, and they have a legal obligation to sell the property to you at the terms set in the contract.

On the flip side of the coin, the buyer (the wholesaler) has power because they now control the property. If the contract is written correctly, they have the power to go and find someone who will fill their shoes as the buyer. In exchange for letting someone else buy this great deal, they will normally be paid a fee.

There are no normal wholesale fees. How much a wholesaler gets paid is dependent on what price they can get the seller to agree to sell them the property at, and how much the property is worth.

An example: Dave is a wholesaler. Dave goes and finds a house on ABC street that looks run down and needs some love. Dave does some research and finds out that Bill owns the house. Dave contacts Bill and tells him that he would like to buy the house. Dave does his research and figures out that the house is worth $100,000 as is, and if fixed up it could be worth $150,000.

Dave tells Bill that he will offer him $50,000. Bill gets angry at first but then tells Dave he will do the deal at $65,000. Dave writes a contract with Bill and they agree to do the transaction for $65,000 in 60 days from signing the contract.

Now Dave goes to an investor he knows, Tom, and tells him about this great deal he has. He tells Tom that the house is worth $100,000 now, and if Tom were to fix it up for $20,000 in repairs, it would be worth $150,000.

He also tells Tom that he will sell him this house today for $90,000 so that Tom will have $10,000 of equity at purchase. (The instant money that Tom makes is the difference between what he buys is for $90,000 and what it is worth today $100,000) This sounds like a great deal to Tom and it is what he is looking for, so he agrees.

Tom pays Dave $90,000 and then Dave gives Bill $65,000. Everyone is happy!

Dave never has to buy the house or put up any money. He simply "assigns" this contract to Tom for $90,000. Dave now gets a profit of $90,000-$65,000 = $25,000!

This is one example. The profit on these deals can be much smaller, with some being much bigger.

PROS:
- No/little money needed
- Quick cash
- Can do this anywhere in the US with internet and cell phone

CONS:
- One time money
- Risk that "Tom" falls through and you make no money
- Treated as regular income
- No tax benefits
- You are still working a job. This is not investing. If you stop working, you stop making money

CHAPTER 15

FLIPPING PROPERTIES

You are most likely already familiar with flipping, but let's spend a quick second on flipping to understand why it is not investing.

The process of flipping is buying a property that is outdated and needs work. Once the work is done, you hope that the value of the property has increased by more than you spent on the improvements. Let's define a few keywords.

ARV stands for After Repair Value. This is what the flipper can sell the house for after it is fixed up.

Closing costs are what we, as a property owner, will pay when we are selling a property. Standard commissions to an agent in residential is 5%-6% of the purchase price, paid by the person selling the property. Also we will have to pay legal fees, which we can estimate at 1% for the sake of this example.

Who pays what closing costs and legal fees depend on what state and county you are in. Each county will have a standard split of what the buyer pays and what the seller pays, but this is all negotiable in your transaction. Some examples of closing costs include title search, and transaction fees to pay the attorney or title company for their time spent helping you buy or sell the property.

These fees mean that if we sell a house for $100,000 then we are only going to walk away with $93,000 because we had $7,000 (7%) of fees we had to pay.

Rehab budget is how much the flipper anticipates spending on the materials and labor (such as countertops, new roofs, new floors, paint, labor and permit fees from the city if applicable). Depending on what kind of condition the house is in and how nice you want to make the house will determine how much the rehab budget will need to be.

Holding costs are the expenses we are going to have to pay for owning a property. These costs include power bills, water bills, property insurance, property taxes and other costs that come with property ownership. The longer you own a property, the more in holding costs you are going to have.

The final piece we need to understand is **profit**. This is how much the flipper would like to make from the transaction after all expenses are paid.

The flipper should buy the property according to the following formula:

ARV - closing costs - rehab budget - holding cost - Profit = Purchase price

If a flipper follows the above formula, they will know how much to pay for a property when a wholesaler or agent comes to them with a potential property they can buy.

Pro Tip: leave yourself at least a 30% profit margin as a flipper. Do not cut your profit short. If the deal doesn't work, it doesn't work. DO NOT BEND YOUR RULES. Move on to the next deal and pass up deals with thin margins. If you run into unexpected expenses you did not plan for (which you will) you do not want to be working to flip a house with no profit for yourself at the end.

Flipping a house is not investing in real estate because you are actively working on a project until it is finished. Then, to make a profit, you have to sell the product. You will only make money from a house flip when you successfully sell the property to someone else.

This is no different than what any product based business does. They build a product, and then in order to make money off of it, they have to sell it. If you do not sell the product, you make no money! With house flipping, the longer you hold the house without selling it, the less money you will profit because your holding costs are going to rise. This is normal business, and it is not a bad way to do things, but we must realize that this is a different model and strategy than investing.

Please do not confuse flipping for profits with investing that will build long term wealth and monthly cash flow.

First time flipper mistake: Most first time house flippers think that they are going to do all the work themselves, and make an extra profit because they are not going to pay a professional to fix the toilets or install new flooring. Often people will have to do the work themselves to make the numbers work, and come out with a profit. What most people overlook in the equation is the value of their own time.

If you are an accountant that can make $50 an hour, you would be doing yourself a disservice by working on a house flip. You may think you are going to save money by doing the work yourself instead of hiring a company or person to do it for you. Painting is not hard, anyone can do it, including you. So why pay someone when you can do it yourself?

If your best skill is being an accountant, then you should do accounting at $50 an hour because you can hire someone to paint for you at $15 an hour. By painting yourself, you are really losing $50 - $15 = $35 every hour that you spend painting instead of accounting.

One of the "x factors" that leads to high drop out rate in house flipping is that when you have a day job and you are trying to flip a house is the amount of frustration that you will run into. You work all day from 9-5 and then you go to work on your flip from 5-11 pm at night. Your quality of work is not as good as a professional, but you think doing it yourself will be cheaper.

You also really want to get the flip completed to get your payday, so you spend all day Saturday and Sunday working on completing the flip. This goes on for several months, and you quickly become exhausted and fed up with flipping. You haven't seen your friends, you haven't had a social life, haven't watched a game, haven't had quality time with your significant other.

Eventually you get the house done, put it on the market after months of laboring, for it to sit on the market and wait. Your holding costs rise to where they begin to eat into your profit. You grow nervous so you drop the price in hopes that it will sell faster.

The flip formula for people who do it themselves looks like this:

ARV - closing costs - rehab budget - holding cost - their time - purchase price = Profit

When you do any of the physical work yourself, you need to factor your time into the equation so you find out if you are actually making any money, or if you would actually have a loss instead of a profit when being paid for your time on other activities.

This is the unfortunate story of most first time house flippers, and I do not want this for you. You need to invest your money one time, and get paid a profit each and every month for the rest of your life, without having to labor.

When you *shift from house flipping for a profit to real estate investing for a monthly cash flow*, you put yourself in a position to build incredible wealth, have free time, and live a quality life doing the things you want to do!

There is so much more to house flipping that we could talk about, but the purpose of this section is for you to realize that house flipping can be profitable, but it is less stable and will not make you wealthy like commercial investing for cash flow will. Let's spend our time together educating you on acquiring assets that put cash in your pocket consistently and forever.

PROS:

- Profitable if done right

CONS:

- Requires cash
- One time money. Only get paid when the property sells
- Taxed as regular income if done under a year
- No tax benefits
- Not investing
- Dependent on end buyer to get paid
- Can take long periods of time
- Dependent on real estate values to make money
- Real estate market can change while you are in the middle of your flip

CHAPTER 16

BEING AN AGENT

When you read the previous section on flipping, you might have been surprised to find such a big part of your property sales proceeds go to real estate commissions. This is why so many people get their real estate license and try to become a realtor.

A realtor has the potential to make a lot of money by selling other people's properties for them, or by helping a home buyer or investor find the property they would like to buy. There are two different kinds of realtors.

The first is the listing agent, who represents the current property owner who is trying to sell their property.

The next kind of agent represents the property buyers, who are looking for a property to buy.

The realtors or brokers on the transaction are responsible for representing their clients throughout the entire process and telling them what they should be cautious of and how the entire buying or selling process works. The truth is many people do not understand very simple things about real estate such as what the title is, what due diligence is and why it is important, and what it means for earnest money to go hard. This is where an agent should guide you, and this is why they get paid. My goal for you as an investor is to know all this yourself.

In exchange for their efforts, the realtors are typically each paid 2.5-3% of the sales price as a commission. Both sides of the commission are normally paid by the property seller in a typical real estate sale. If it is a larger transaction, the property seller may negotiate with the listing agent to pay a 4% (2% to each agent) instead of 6%. Or instead, the seller may tell the agent that they only want to pay the listing agent a commission, and if the buyers agent wants to get paid, the buyer is going to have to pay them themselves.

There are no set in stone rules on commission, but there are norms in the industry.

To calculate how much an agent can make off a transaction, simply multiply their commission percentage by the sales price. A 3% commission on a $100,000 house would be a $3,000 payday. A 3% commission on a $1,000,000 house would be a $30,000 payday.

Many people who go and get their license look at these numbers and tell themselves, "If I can just sell a few $1,000,000 houses a year, I'm doing better than I am at my current job!" But what many people who dive in head first don't realize is that the realtor business is a relationship business, not a real estate business.

To get listings or to represent a buyer on a transaction, you must have a relationship with the property seller or buyer. It can take years and years to build the kind of strong, quality relationships you need in order to have a big, vibrant book of business you need to make a lot of money as a realtor. You can certainly do it, but most people think once they get their license the business will pour in, and it doesn't happen.

Another thing to consider is how long it can take to make money. Once you list a property, or start to look for property for a buyer, you could spend weeks or months finding the right property or person to buy your listing. Once you do find that person, you have to negotiate the terms. Then you have to have the contract signed. Once the contract is signed, it could take another 2-3 months for the property to close, and then you will finally get paid. That is a long time and a lot of work in order to get your first paycheck.

Being an agent is a full time job that I would classify as a service-based business rather than a real estate business. The best agents serve their clients to the highest degree and that is why they are successful.

PROS:

- Little money needed to get in
- Can make a lot of money off of other people's properties

CONS:

- Can take a long time to make money
- Not as easy as everyone thinks
- Not investing
- No tax benefits
- Have to get license and register under a broker to get started
- Share your commission with broker

Pro Tip: If you are selling a property, I would recommend paying the normal commission to your agent, as you want to have your interests as a seller aligned with both agents. If you try to skimp your realtor on their commission, are they really going to fight hard to get you the maximum price from a seller? If you tell the other side that you are not going to pay them, will they bring their buyer to your property, or will they tell their buyer that your deal is not as good as the one down the road (that happens to have a commission in it for them)?

CHAPTER 17

RESIDENTIAL INVESTING

Investing in homes is how many people get started building true wealth in real estate. It was my first cash flow investment. A house makes sense to most people, and it does not present too much of a mental roadblock because we can all wrap our heads around a house.

A popular and easy route that most people take when they get started is to buy a home to live in. Once they move out, instead of selling the house they will rent it out. Because they are going to live in it for some time, this is called an "owner occupant". The owner occupant qualifies for some great financing programs that don't require a lot of cash to get started.

The government wants you to own a house. If you own a house, you will have a house payment, property taxes, and the general ownership of that house will boost the economy. You will also want to have a job so that you can make these payments each month. When a toilet breaks, you call a plumber. When the roof has a leak, you call a roofer. Remember what you learned earlier? A house is going to take money out of your pocket!

Home ownership leads to more dollars exchanging hands in the economy, and that is what the government wants. So they incentivize banks to give out special mortgages that make it very easy for most people to become a homeowner.

There are some programs out there where you can get into a house for $0 down. That means if you buy a house for $100,000, the bank will give you all $100,000. The majority of programs do require you to have some skin in the game and put down 3-5% of the purchase price, so $3,000-$5,000 on a $100,000 house.

With programs like these out there, there are many people who have built their real estate investments up by buying a house with little to no money of their own. Once they meet the qualifications of living there for a year, they move out and rent the house to a tenant and go buy another one to repeat the process.

This is the big shift from house flipping to real investing!

The way we make money off of rental property is by collecting rents from the tenants, paying the expenses, paying the bank our monthly payment, and then at the end of each month we have money left over to keep for ourselves.

Here is what a house investment would look like every month:

Rental income = $1,800
Insurance = $200
Property taxes = $300
Mortgage = $1,100

Now we figure out how much we are going to make.

Rental income - insurance - property taxes - mortgage = profit

$1,800 - $200 - $300 - $1,100 = $200

This would be called a profit and loss statement (P&L for short). We can take this simple equation and turn it to look like this:

Income:
Rental income　　$ 1,800

Expense:
Insurance　　　　$ -200
Property Taxes　　$ -300
Mortgage　　　　$-1,100
Profit　　　　　　$　200

In business we call income - expenses = profit, in real estate we call it rental income - expenses = cash flow.

The investor is making $200 a month from that house, and he is having his mortgage paid at the same time. We call this cash flow positive when the income from the rent is greater than all the expenses and you have a profit at the end of the month.

We will go deeper into how a mortgage works in a later chapter, but understand that by paying that mortgage every month, the investor is making money there too. Each month the amount owed to the bank goes down.

Now consider if the investor did this once a year for the next 5 years. The investor would now own 5 homes and would be making $1,000 extra a month without a large time obligation every month. Each month 5 mortgages would be paid down by your tenants for you.

If $1,000 a month doesn't sound great to you, don't worry. This is just the beginning. It gets much better!

The key here is to make sure that the amount you can rent a house for is greater than the expenses. You do not want your rental income to be less than your expenses. At that point you are paying for someone else to live in your house, and your cash flow positive *asset* becomes a cash flow negative *liability*.

Asset = Something that puts money in your pocket

Liability = Something that takes money out of your pocket

The beautiful thing about real estate investing is that it does not require a lot of ongoing time and effort on behalf of the property owner once you know what you are doing. Think about this for yourself when you have rented a place for your personal housing. How often did you contact the landlord? Probably only once a month when you had to pay rent.

As a property owner, you are on the flip side of that equation. Most of the time, you only hear from a tenant when they are paying their rent.

There are many things you can do as a landlord to properly and legally screen potential tenants to make sure they are good people and will not be a pain in your neck while they live in your house. That is a major key to residential investing—make sure you have great tenants! The tenants you allow to live in your house will either make your life amazing, or make it hell. Do your proper research before letting someone move in.

The idea of buying one house and renting it for cash flow and then doing this again to build more cash flow is what in real estate we call the snowball effect. Once you have 1 house, things move slow because you are waiting to qualify for the next low money down loan. You are also waiting on your bank account to fill back up so you can spend your excess money on your next investment. As time goes on, your monthly cash flow builds up more and more and you begin to have your bank account fill up quicker and quicker. This reduces the time between each of your investments and grows at a faster rate each time. Like a snowball, it gets bigger and goes faster when it goes down a hill.

This is how most people get started, and it has made many people wealthier than they ever could have become by just working a normal job.

Most people are also saying to themselves right now, "Yea, and in addition to making that $200 profit every month and the mortgage being paid down, the house is going to rise in value over time!" Agreed, and that is where a lot of wealth is built, but one of the main points for you to take away from this book will be explained in depth in the next chapter. You will really need to pay attention in the next chapter to fully understand why residential investing is good, but not the best path for true wealth.

Also, by betting on the house value to rise, we are not practicing good fundamentals of investing! You shouldn't invest in a house that has $0 of cash flow each month just because you think the value of the house will go up. This is gambling! My personal rule is that I will not invest in a property unless it is cash flow positive. We hope and think the value of the investment will go up over time, but we should only bet on that if we have cash flow.

In addition to the house value going up in time, your tenants paying off your mortgage for you, and putting money in your pocket every month, you get amazing tax benefits for renting out a house too. We will go into all the different tax benefits in Section 7.

A simple example of the tax benefits for now: if you buy a house for $100,000 and make it a rental property, you will get to take that $100,000 and "depreciate" it over the next 27.5 years. $100,000 divided by 27.5 comes out to $3,636. That means that every year, you could profit $3,636 and not have to pay any taxes on that profit. Pretty amazing!

Notice how in the example you made $200 a month, coming out to $2,400 in a year. With depreciation that would mean you keep all the $2,400 without paying ANY TAXES on it, and you have an extra $1,236 of depreciation that you can use to shield other income you make from your regular job.

This is a small example to show you one tax break real estate investors get, but this is just the start of the amazing powers of real estate provides. We will also talk about how you get to write off the interest you pay on your mortgage. Again, more on this in section 7.

Investing in residential real estate is true investing unlike any of the above methods, but it gets better than this.

PROS:

- Monthly cash flow
- Home value increase long term
- Tenants pay off mortgage
- Use bank's money to buy your house
- Low and no money down programs
- Tax benefits
- Residual income with little effort

CONS:

- Tenant risk
- Slow snowball
- Small amounts of cash flow

CHAPTER 18

COMMERCIAL INVESTING

Commercial real estate investing follows the same exact blueprint as residential: make sure the money you receive from rents is more than the money you have to pay for expenses. The difference here is that instead of a house we may have an office building, a shopping center, a gas station, a grocery store, a medical building, an apartment complex, a self storage complex, a hotel, a golf course, a vacation resort, a car wash, or even a piece of land we rent out.

As you can see there are many different types of commercial real estate, but the ways you can make money off of them are the same. We always want to analyze the property before we buy it to make sure that it is going to be cash flow positive. This is called "underwriting" and you will learn about it in this book. Underwriting is an *essential skill* for an investor.

Many residential investors never graduate to commercial investing, which is a shame. There is no secret to investing in commercial real estate, and again you do not have to have any sort of license or degree to invest in commercial real estate.

Every commercial investor I have talked to about their experience says the same thing when I ask them what their biggest mistake has been. They always answer immediately, "waiting too long to get started on bigger deals!"

To repeat, commercial investing is no different than residential investing. The biggest difference is that you are going to make larger sums of money in commercial.

There are a few differences that are worth noting and learning about.

In commercial real estate investing, we will not be able to get as good of a loan from the bank. If we buy a property for $1,000,000, we are generally going to be able to get between $750,000 - $800,000 for that property from the bank, and we are going to have come up with the rest of that cash. We are not able to get as good of a loan on commercial properties as we can on residential because banks are not incentivized by the government to give out awesome loans.

Banks know that commercial real estate is not somewhere we are going to live, and generally it is an investment. If an investment goes bad, people are much more likely to walk away from an investment than they are their home where they live. For this reason, the banks want us to have a larger amount of our own money in the deal, so we are less likely to walk away if things get rocky.

They also want the amount of cash the property produces to be more than enough to cover the cost of the expenses and mortgage. This ensures they will always get paid.

While this seems like an obstacle for those of you who do not have that much cash, please do not turn off your brain and put this book back on the shelf. You are about to learn ways to overcome this and get started investing in commercial properties to make your cash flow snowball grow bigger, faster.

The next section is going to take a deep dive into the comparison between residential and commercial, so we will continue this section there. We will talk about how commercial real estate is less risky than residential and how there is less emotion involved. This is good for you. Use the below pros section as a reference for what is to come in the next section.

PROS:

- Much larger profit potential
- Control what your property is worth based on income
- Enough income to delegate all ongoing responsibilities
- Multiple tenants = Income diversification
- Greater value add opportunity

CONS:

- Scary for new investors
- More cash needed for purchase

CHAPTER 19

DEVELOPMENT

Let's briefly touch on property development. Development consists of taking a piece of land and building on it. You can develop condos, apartments, medical offices, etc.

Anything you see that is not a raw piece of land has been a development project at one time.

Property development is a great way to take an underutilized piece of property and maximize its potential. Most people think that property developers take a raw piece of land and build a building on it and sell it right when it is built. This is only one type of property development.

I will not advocate for or against this strategy, but will say that it is not true real estate investing if you are developing a property with the intent to sell it once it is built. If you are doing this, you are doing the same thing as flipping a house with a slight variation. House flipping is essentially a form of redevelopment.

On the other hand, if you are developing a property with the intention of holding it to rent out and create cash flow for yourself once it is completed, this is investing and can be a great way to create amazing deals. Even when the real estate market is hot and prices are sky high, making it difficult to find a good cash flow property to buy where the numbers make sense, development can create great deals.

Most people hear the horror stories of 2008 and how so many property developers went bankrupt and automatically assume any sort of development is risky.

I am in the middle of developing a project right now and I do not view the project as risky. Here's why: The developers that got crushed in 2008 were taking out large loans on their projects that depended on their projects selling to be repaid. Think about a subdivision or a condo project. In order to receive income from these projects, the developers had to sell their units to a buyer.

Their business model was to sell the units for hundreds of thousands of dollars. Once they paid off their loan, they would have mountains of profits and life would be good. Well when they borrowed money in 2007 and everything was great, they had no problem borrowing all that money. Real estate was at the highest price it had ever been and could only go up, right?

WRONG.

The prices of the product they were developing dropped and many of the buyers went away. The developers were now left with a product they could not sell, and their debts on the project were due.

Where did they go wrong?

Well, hindsight is always 20/20, but if these developers had gotten long term debt and were building products that were planned on being rented monthly instead of being sold 1 time, they would have had a much better chance of making it through the recession.

Did you know that most self storage and apartment buildings actually increased in value and produced more income during the recession? That's right! Some real estate actually performed BETTER during the recession. Not all forms of real estate behave the same.

So let's come back around to the project I am doing. My project will have long term debt on it that will not be due for 7 years. I am building a product that is going to rent forever, instead of selling one time.

I have also reduced my risk in this project because I have started to prelease the space, meaning I have customers ready to pay me before I actually spend any money on the construction.

Is this making sense? Do you see how there are 2 sides of the coin when it comes to real estate development? There is going to be risk in any venture, but <u>it is up to you</u> to reduce your risk as much as possible, and that starts with educating yourself.

PROS:
- Make a lot of money if done right
- Build your desired investment where you want it, how you want it

CONS:
- Many moving parts
- Long process
- Uncertainty
- Requires education
- Not always investing depending on business plan and strategy

BENEFITS OF REAL ESTATE DEEP DIVE

So you have read some benefits about different positions in real estate, but it is of utmost importance that you understand this section and what makes real estate so great. With the factor of many moving pieces, you need to understand each component of what makes real estate such an attractive investment. Let's do a deep dive on each aspect!

CHAPTER 20

CASH FLOW IS KING

Personally, this is my favorite part of real estate! Cash flow as we described above when the income from the rent is greater than the expenses and mortgage payments on a property. This leaves you with excess money at the end of each month to put in your pocket.

If you are a landlord, you love the 1st of the month because that's when rent is due, and that means you are getting another round of cash flow no matter where you are in the world, or what you are doing.

Robert Kiyosaki talks about how he had $50,000 and wanted to get a Porsche, but he didn't want to spend all his cash on the car. He knew the car was going to go down in value once he started driving it. If he had just bought the car with the money, it would have looked like this:

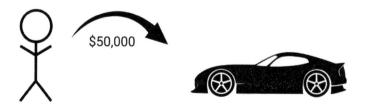

This would take money out of his pocket, and would be a liability.

So instead of spending his money on the car, he went out and bought an investment property with the $50,000. He then went and got a loan on the car. Now he had an asset that produced monthly cash flow that made his car payments for him, and put extra gas money in his pocket each month! He used an asset to pay for a liability! This is what the rich do.

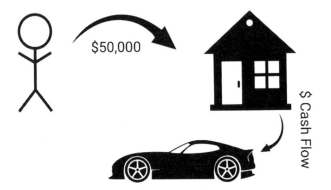

He used the power of cash flow to get himself a free Porsche. He did not have to make the monthly payments, he let his property make the payments for him! Cash flow is the gift that keeps on giving each and every month. Once you own an investment property, you get paid every month for the rest of your life through cash flow.

After the car was paid off, he now had a free car and his property was going to start paying him directly instead of paying for his car payment.

Cash flow format:

Income - expenses - debt = cash flow

Or in P&L format:

   Income
  - Expenses
  - Debt
  = Cash flow

Cash flow is residual income. It is doing work one time and getting paid forever for it. Of course there is a small amount of work you will have to do every month. But, the majority of your time and effort will be up front for the project, and then once you own it you have a predictable income stream forever!

Your goal should be to trade the cash you have now for cash flow in the future.

To build wealth you need to know that *cash flow is better than cash.*

Cash flow > Cash

Once you switch from working for money at a job or flipping houses for a profit to earning residual cash flow, you have reached investor status and will join the ranks of the wealthy very quickly.

CHAPTER 21

PROPERTY APPRECIATION

S ome investors would argue with me that appreciation is better than cash flow! I love appreciation but will not invest unless there is cash flow in a property first and foremost.

Appreciation is a fancy word to describe an increase in a property value. We have seen tremendous amounts of appreciation in real estate from 2010 to 2020. If you purchased a piece of property for $100,000 5 years ago and today you could sell it for $150,000, it would have appreciated $50,000 or 50%. With this being said, appreciation is not guaranteed from year to year, but over time property values have gone up in the long run. Appreciation can occur for many reasons.

The first is inflation. Every year, the value of the dollar is supposed to go down by 2%. That is the target set by the Federal Reserve. If the value of the dollar goes down, the value of real estate goes up. This means that a house that was worth $100,000 *should be* worth $102,000 by the same day next year. The year after that it should be worth $104,040 (1.02 X $102,000). Did the house really go up in value, or did the value of the dollar decrease? Either way, the value of your properties are going to go up relative to the dollar over time. This is inflation.

The next way that properties appreciate is through supply and demand. If you want an extreme example of this, look in the Bay Area of California. There are so many people that want to live in that area that real estate prices have gone through the roof. You will be hard pressed to find a nice home in that area for under $1 million. So when you buy in an area that people are moving to and there is a lot of competition for that piece of property, whether it be residential or commercial, you will find that prices go up and you benefit from appreciation.

The best way for you to take advantage of appreciation is to *force it*. In real estate, there is a type of investing called "value-add investing."

Just like it sounds, you are investing with the intention to add value to the property. You are going to force the property to appreciate. How is this done? Well, in the case of a residential property you will want to make it a more desirable place to live, so people will pay you more in rent for it. You could change out the old countertops with new granite countertops, tear out some walls, add some landscaping to make it look nice like the people on TV do.

This is what house flippers do, but you can do it to increase the rents you will receive from the property, thereby increasing the value of it. There is a whole chapter coming up on commercial value add but here is a little sneak peek.

Commercial real estate is valued based off of how much income it produces after the expenses.

Income ↑ = value of property ↑

So in order to force appreciation and drive up how much the property is worth, we need to find a way to either increase the amount of income we receive, decrease expenses, or do both. By making a property look and feel nicer, we can generally charge more in rent for it, increase the income, and from there we will have a property that has appreciated.

This is the kind of appreciation real investors love. If you can assemble a business plan to force appreciation and you have cash flow at the time of purchase, you have a great deal on your hands!

CHAPTER 22

USE YOUR INVESTMENT

Real estate as we talked about earlier while comparing it to stocks is awesome because you can touch it and you can use it. Your piece of real estate will always carry some utility and benefit.

If the price of it drops, did your real estate really become less valuable? In the crash of 2008, when the value of houses dropped, did those houses really become less valuable?

On paper they did, but did a house lose its square footage and become smaller?

Did the granite countertops become less stable?

Did the roof on the house start to leak and allow water to come in?

Did you lose a bedroom and have to kick a roommate out because there wasn't enough space in the house?

Of course not! Real estate is amazing because it has profit potential but it also has real world benefits that will make your life better.

That is why real estate will always be worth something, no matter what happens—because it is usable and has utility.

CHAPTER 23

GROW YOUR EQUITY

Different than appreciation, we have equity building up in our property each month that comes from a reduced loan balance.

Equity is the difference between what a property is worth and how much we owe on that property.

Property Value - Debt = Equity

Year 1: $100,000 - $80,000 = $20,000

As your debt goes down, the amount of money you have in the property goes up, even if the actual value of the property doesn't go up.

This benefit comes from your tenants paying your mortgage bill each month. Each time they pay rent, they are paying for the mortgage instead of you. Some of this money will go towards interest, but other goes towards paying down the amount owed to the bank.

If you buy a property, make your loan payment each month for 5 years, then sell the property for the same amount you bought if for, you will walk away with a profit because you now owe less money to the bank than you did when you first bought the property.

Property Value - Debt = Equity

Year 5: $100,000 - $60,000 = $40,000

You made $20,000 but the value of the property did not go up at all.

By the way, that money is not considered a profit, so you get to keep it tax free!

CHAPTER 24

MAKE INFLATION YOUR FRIEND

A real estate investor's best friend!

Inflation is a secret tax the government puts on us without us realizing it. Each year they want your dollar to decrease in value by 2%. They do this by putting more money into the economy each year. When the fed prints money, the dollars you have become less valuable because there are more of them in the system. As the rules of supply and demand tell us, the more of something there is, the less valuable it is.

We can't do anything to stop this and to stop the dollars in our bank account from becoming less valuable each and everyday. But, we can use this to our advantage.

You see, when you borrow money from a bank, they tell you what your payment is going to be each month for the next 15 to 30 years. You can then use that money, whose payment amount is at a fixed rate, to go and buy cash flow producing real estate. When you buy real estate the right way, you are going to have cash flow at the end of each month. Now you own a product that you sell to your customers every month. You are selling them space, that is your product.

Well, just like the price of milk or gas goes up with inflation, so does rent. The amount your customers are going to pay you each month for your space will go up over time as a result of inflation.

Let's say you own and rent out a house for $1,000 a month, your expenses are $200 a month, and the payment to the bank is $400 a month. That will put your monthly cash flow from the property at $400 a month, or $4,800 a year.

Year	Income	Expenses	Debt	Cash Flow/ Month	Cash Flow/ Year
1	$1,000	$200	$400	$400	$4,800

Let's also say that inflation is 2% a year. Your rent is going to increase, and your expenses are going to increase. But, your debt (your biggest expense) is going to stay the same. Because you lock in your debt payments when you first get a loan, that amount is not going to go up with inflation! Let's look at your cash flow projections:

Year	Income	Expenses	Debt	Cash Flow/ Month	Cash Flow/ Year
1	$1,000	$200	$400	$400	$4,800
2	$1,020	$204	$400	$416	$4,992

As you can see, from year one to year 2, our income increases by 2%, our expenses increase by 2%, but our debt payment stays the same. This results in our monthly cash flow going up by 4%!

Take a look at the power of using inflation to increase rents, and locking in your bank payment over a 10 year period.

Year	Income	Expenses	Debt	Cash Flow/ Month	Cash Flow/ Year
1	$1,000	$200	$400	$400	$4,800
2	$1,020	$204	$400	$416	$4,992
3	$1,040	$208	$400	$432	$5,188
4	$1,061	$212	$400	$449	$5,388
5	$1,082	$216	$400	$466	$5,591
6	$1,104	$221	$400	$483	$5,799
7	$1,126	$225	$400	$501	$6,011
8	$1,149	$230	$400	$519	$6,227
9	$1,172	$234	$400	$537	$6,448
10	$1,195	$239	$400	$556	$6,673

Notice in the chart about how your rent and your expenses increase every year, but your debt payments stay the same. Most people ignore this, but it is one of the most powerful features of real estate investing.

What you have done by borrowing bank money and putting it into cash flow real estate is put yourself on the right side of inflation. The bank does not get a larger payment when inflation occurs, but as a real estate owner you get benefit from rising rents, and more cash flow each year.

Now, not only are you winning because your cash flow is going to increase every year, but you have also taken the winning side of inflation due to your debt going down every year, and the value of your property increases. Again, the difference between what your property is worth and how much you owe on it is called "Equity".

Property Value - Debt = Equity

Let's say you buy a house for $100,000 using a financing program that allows you to use none of your own money. In the beginning, you will owe exactly what the property is worth, and you will have no equity. It will be all debt.

Property value - Debt = Equity

$100,000 - $100,000 = $0

Take a look at the next chart showing how your inflation impacts your equity:

Year	Property Value	Debt	Equity in the property
1	$100,000	$100,000	$0

What happens after a year passes and we own the home? The first thing is the home value is going to rise by 2% due to inflation, but we are also going to have the debt reduced on the property. Look at the chart:

Year	Property Value	Debt	Equity in the property
1	$100,000	$100,000	$0
2	$102,000	$98,000	$4,000

We made a total of $4,000 in equity in two ways. First we made $2,000 by the value of the property going up. Next we made $2,000 by the amount we owe the bank going down.

Take a look at the power of this over a 10 year time period:

Year	Property Value	Debt	Equity in the property
1	$100,000	$100,000	$0
2	$102,000	$98,000	$4,000
3	$104,040	$96,000	$8,040
4	$106,121	$94,000	$12,121
5	$108,243	$92,000	$16,243
6	$110,408	$90,000	$20,408
7	$112,616	$88,000	$24,616
8	$114,869	$86,000	$28,869
9	$117,166	$84,000	$33,166
10	$119,509	$82,000	$37,509

In this example, if you would have bought a property for $100,000 and borrowed all the money to buy it, in 10 years you would have $37,509. This is the difference in what the property is worth, and what you owe to the bank. This is your money! Again, this is what we call equity.

Not only did you enjoy the cash flow, but you also are building up a large amount of equity, because you put yourself on the right side of inflation!

This is extremely powerful. The combination of inflation pushing equity and cash flow is why so much wealth is built in real estate.

*Please note, debt does not go down in a straight line like this chart shows. We used round numbers here for a simple illustration. Section 8 will explain how debt decreases over time.

Before the year 2000, people who saved money were smart. They were winners because they saved money, put it in the bank and earned a good rate of return.

Today we are operating under old advice that is no longer useful. In fact, saving money is a bad thing to do these days, and it is what the financially uneducated are doing. If you want to learn more about why savers are now losers, visit HaydenCrabtree.com/resources to watch a quick video of exactly what this means. The rules of the game have changed and most people aren't aware of why they are losing without realizing it.

The intention of this section was to open your eyes to all the different ways real estate benefits its owners. We are going to examine these topics to get a better understanding of their true power and to give you more detail.

Were you aware of all these different benefits?

These benefits are the reason the rich are getting richer, and the poor are getting poorer.

These benefits of real estate are one reason the divide between the rich and the poor is larger than it has ever been. Put yourself on the right side of this equation, take advantage of these 7 benefits, and become wealthy!

SECTION 5

RESIDENTIAL VS COMMERCIAL

OVERVIEW

This is my favorite chapter. The real reason behind writing this book and calling it *Skip The Flip* is because I talk to so many people on a weekly basis who want to get into real estate investing. But these people are misguided. They think they should flip a house and that will make them investors. They do not have their attention in the correct niche. If they could absorb the information in this book, they would put themselves 5-10 years ahead of where they are now, and shorten the learning curve to real estate success. My goal is to shorten your timeframe and help you become successful quicker.

The advice "there are no shortcuts to success" is bad advice. There are shortcuts to success in this world. By reading this book, you are taking a shortcut. By finding a mentor, you are taking a shortcut. This chapter is a real estate investing shortcut that will save time, money and energy.

Residential real estate is where many people get their start because it is easier. Commercial real estate seems to have this mental roadblock for most people and few ever push into the bigger properties. This chapter is going to tell you why you should skip residential and go straight for bigger, commercial properties and how doing so will increase your investing success.

On my YouTube channel, I post weekly educational videos to help you grow your real estate portfolio. If you are enjoying this book, go over to YouTube and search "Hayden Crabtree" and subscribe to my channel!

CHAPTER 25

COMMERCIAL VS RESIDENTIAL RISK

A main take away for you to remember is that commercial real estate has less risk than residential does.

In commercial real estate, you can reduce your risk by having many tenants instead of one tenant. In residential real estate such as a house, you have one customer. You are relying on one tenant to pay your rent. In commercial real estate, you have many tenants. This drastically reduces your risk because your income is coming from different sources.

Think about it this way: If you have expenses of $200 and a mortgage payment of $600, that's $800 a month in expenses. If your tenant pays rent of $1,000, you make a positive $200 in cash flow. This is a 20% margin.

But what does your life look like when the unexpected happens?

What if your tenant loses their job, gets injured, or moves out? Who is going to pay the $800 a month in expenses?

That's right, *you are.*
This is a risk, so how do we reduce our risk?

Let's look at a commercial property, say a 100 unit apartment complex. The apartment complex now has 100 tenants instead of 1.

You now have diversified your income source. Now you are not relying on 1 person to pay your expenses for you, instead you are relying on 100 people. What happens if 1 person moves out, 1 person gets injured, and another loses their job?

These 3 people may not pay you, but the other 97 will pay. You will have all your expenses paid for and still get some positive cash flow in your pocket.

Like the example of one house where you have a 20% margin, you will also have a 20% margin on the larger 100 unit complex. That would come out to $20,000 a month in positive cash flow. In this case, if you had 3 people not pay their rent, you would not make $20,000, but you would still make $17,000 in cash flow.

By adding volume to your income, and having income coming in from many sources, you have some room in your profit margin for unexpected things to happen, and still have cash flow.

The reality of investing is that you have to deal with people, and some people in this world do not live up to their promises, or they have bad things happen inside of their own life that causes them to not perform the way they should. That does not mean you shouldn't get started investing because sometimes people aren't going to pay. What it does mean is that you should be aware of the risks and prepare your strategy accordingly.

By buying properties that rely on 10 or more tenants instead of 1, you have reduced your risk of having to pay for the expenses out of your pocket when a tenant or two doesn't make their rent payment.

This is a major key that many first time investors overlook when they decide to rent out their first house. They get discouraged when it sits vacant for a month or two and nobody rents it. They get down on themselves when their tenant runs into financial hardship and can't make the rent payment and they, as the owner of the property, still have to make the power, insurance and property tax payment.

Be aware of this pitfall from the start and protect yourself from this risk by investing in properties that have a diverse income source in multiple tenants.

CHAPTER 26

ADD "A PLAYERS" TO YOUR TEAM

The next reason you should invest in commercial over residential is because of how much more income the properties bring in. This is not just a benefit because you will make more money, but you can also spread the love around.

When your property only brings in $1,000-$2,000 a month, you can't afford to hire anyone full time to help you manage that property. Hiring anyone is going to cost more than what you can afford because any salary or wages you pay is going to eat into your cash flow. This means you have to do everything yourself. Not good.

Trust me, life is much better as an investor when you can have other people help manage your properties and take on responsibilities for you. That is the whole point of investing, being able to do what you want and *have your money work for you.*

If you have a 100 unit apartment complex, at $1,000 rent per unit, that property will be bringing in around $100,000 a month. Now your expenses and debt payments will be much bigger. At this scale you will be able to afford to pay someone $5,000 a month to be a manager on the property for you. This will allow you to go look for another property to buy instead of having to watch over the property all the time. In residential real estate, you are going to have to pay people less, and therefore will not be able to hire high quality people who can help you grow your business.

A key lesson to learn not just in real estate but in any business is that people always come first. No matter what you are doing, you are going to have to deal with people. You want to surround yourself with high quality, smart people who can help you on your mission.

CHAPTER 27

CONTROL YOUR VALUE

What is the difference between how residential real estate and commercial real estate is valued? How do we determine how much we could sell the property for?

Residential real estate is valued based off of supply and demand. Essentially, what someone who wants to live in a house is willing to pay for it is what it is worth. You could have the same exact house, but if the house is in North Dakota, it is going to be worth far less money than it would be if it were in Beverly Hills, California, or Manhattan in New York City. This is because less people want to live in North Dakota than Beverly Hills or Manhattan.

It's the same house, but there are more people wanting to live there, therefore the demand is higher and the price is higher.

Same house, different value.

But how is commercial real estate valued?

The next chapter takes a deep dive into this, but the short answer is that commercial real estate is valued off of how much money it makes. That's because commercial real estate is an investment. It is less emotional, and more of a business decision.

If we can raise the income of a commercial property, it is going to be worth more.

Period. No debating that fact.

However if we redo a kitchen in a house, is it going to be worth a predictable amount more? Some will say yes, but at the end of the day it is only going to be worth what the end home buyer wants to pay for it.

The difference in these valuation methods is called income approach vs comparable sales approach. In the income approach, we value the property based on its income. The higher the income, the higher the value. The lower the income, the lower the value.

On the comparable sales approach, we look at properties like ours and see what they are selling for. The problem, to me, with the comparable approach is that the value of my property is determined by other people in other transactions. There is only so much I can do to increase the value of my property. What happens if someone in the other transaction was a bad negotiator and they got a lower price for their house than they should have? That affects the value of my property negatively.

That is why you should choose properties where you can control the income, and thus control the value. Most investors do not understand this key difference when they first start. Most people generally never understand this concept, so congratulations you are ahead of 99% of the population because you read this section.

VALUING COMMERCIAL PROPERTY

Hooray! You now get to learn how to value commercial property. This is a skill that will be valuable for you throughout your entire life. After reading this chapter, you will quickly be able to look at a commercial property for sale and have a good idea of how much the property is worth.

You are also going to learn a little secret that commercial property brokers use to know if you are a rookie or not, and how you can use this to your advantage in purchasing a property.

CHAPTER 28

NET OPERATING INCOME (NOI)

There are 2 main factors that impact the value of commercial real estate. The first is the "Net Operating Income." This will almost always be shortened to "NOI". The NOI of a property is determined by the following formula:

Income - Expenses = Net Operating Income

OR in P&L format:

> Income
> - Expenses
> = Net Operating Income

That's it. The NOI of a property is very easily determined. All we are looking for is income minus expenses.

"Wow, Hayden, it's that easy?! All I have to do is look at the *cash flow* and that will tell me how much the property is worth?!"

"Well, not exactly," I always have to reply, taking the excitement out of whoever I'm talking to. "You see, *cash flow and NOI are not the same thing.* There is one big difference."

CHAPTER 29

CASH FLOW

C ash flow is calculated using the following formula:

Income - Expenses = Net operating income

Net operating income - Debt service* = Cash flow

OR

Income
- Expenses
= Net Operating Income
- Debt Service*
= Cash flow

*Debt service is a fancy word for mortgage payment

Net operating income is valuing the property before we make any debt payments. The reason for this is we do not have to use the bank to help us buy the property. If we want to, and we have enough money, we could use all our own money to buy a property and we would not have to pay the bank anything.

In the case that you do not use a bank, your cash flow WOULD be equal to your NOI. But you miss out on many benefits that real estate provides if you do use a bank's money. You are shooting yourself in the foot and slowing down your business growth if you only use your own money. For that reason, many investors use a lender's money.

"So if almost everyone uses a bank's money, we can come to the same number as a value for the property if we use both NOI and cash flow, right?"

CHAPTER 30

WHY YOU USE NOI INSTEAD OF CASH FLOW FOR VALUE

No, not exactly. If we had identical properties that looked like the following

$100,000 - $40,000 = $60,000 (NOI)

OR

Income	$100,000
Expense	$ -40,000
NOI	$ 60,000

and we have 2 different investors both bought a copy of that property, they could have different cash flows, even though the property has the same NOI and is worth the same amount of money.

Why is that?

Let's say one of the property buyers is you and the other buyer is Warren Buffet. Now, I don't know you, but I would be willing to bet you are not in a better financial position than Warren Buffet.

You see, when we go to the bank, they look at us and ask themselves, "How risky is this person?" If you are risky, they are going to charge you a higher interest rate.

The interest rate is a reflection of risk.

The interest rate is the cost of money. The higher the interest rate, the more you are going to have to pay for the money you borrowed. When the risk is higher, the bank is going to want to make more money for taking on that risk.

So for the 2 borrowers, you and Warren Buffet, who is going to present more risk to the bank? The bank is going to define risk as what are my chances of this money getting repaid on time.

Warren is very low risk because they know he is good for the money. He has a track record of doing well in investing and repaying his debts.

You, on the other hand, present more risk than Warren because you are not a billionaire. That's ok, and you should not get down on yourself for not being a billionaire, you'll get there one day!

For now, you'll have to face the facts that you are going to get a higher interest rate than Warren is. This is not a bad thing, and it does not mean you shouldn't take the bank's money. It is just how finance works. Now back to our example.

Because Warren can get a lower interest rate than you, this is what his cash flow is going to look like

NOI - debt service = cash flow
(NOI) $60,000 - (DS) $10,000 = $50,000 cash flow

OR in P&L format

Income	$ 100,000
Expense	$ -40,000
NOI	$ 60,000
Debt Service	$ -10,000
Cash flow	$ 50,000

On this property, Warren is going to have $10,000 debt payments, and therefore his cash flow is going to be $50,000.

Because you are riskier than Warren, you will have a higher interest rate, but the bank is still going to lend you the money. You borrow the same amount of money as Warren, but your debt payments are $15,000 instead of $10,000. Here is what your cash flow is going to look like

(NOI) $60,000 - (DS) $15,000 = $45,000 cash flow

OR

Income	$100,000
Expense	$ -40,000
NOI	$ 60,000
Debt Service	$ -15,000
Cash flow	$ 45,000

You had to pay $5,000 more than Warren, even though you both borrowed the same amount of money, the property was worth the same amount, and the NOI is the same. The extra $5,000 you paid is because the bank wanted more money from you, because you are more of a risk than Warren.

In finance and investing, there is a general rule that goes as follows:

The higher the risk of a project, the higher return is required.

The lower the risk of a project, the lower return is required.

All this comes back to the whole reason why we use NOI instead of cash flow to value a property. It would not be fair for Warren's property to be worth more just because he is a better borrower in the eyes of the bank than we are. It is the same property, but the cash flows are different because of our personal situation as an investor.

By using the NOI to value the property, we level the playing field for anyone who wants to buy or sell properties. We have to value the property based on the merits and performance of the property itself, not what kind of return it will provide one investor over another.

There is an advantage for investors like Warren. We call this "creditworthy." This means a bank likes to lend to you if you are creditworthy because you are lower risk. For someone who is creditworthy, they are going to be able to achieve a higher cash flow out of the same exact property than someone who is not creditworthy and has to pay a higher interest rate.

Is all this making sense? Do you understand what the NOI is and why we use the NOI instead of cash flow to value a property?

If not then find me on Instagram @HaydenCrabtree and Direct Message what I can help you with. It is crucial you understand NOI before we move on.

To recap:

Net operating income (NOI) = income - expenses.

Cash flow = NOI - debt payments

CHAPTER 31

DETERMINING VALUE

N ow that you understand NOI, you are probably wondering how to use it to determine the value of our property. We will keep the example from above and get rid of our debt service because we don't need that to value a property.

Income	$100,000
Expense	$ -40,000
NOI	$ 60,000

$60,000 is our NOI. First thing to understand is that the NOI is used on an annual basis. There are 2 ways to look at it. If you want you can say what was the income for last year from January 1st to December 31st. The next way to look at it would be for the last 12 months. So if you were in July of 2019, you would look at June 2018–June 2019.

The advantage of doing it this way is you will see the most recent numbers of a property instead of dated numbers. I prefer to look at the trailing 12 months instead of January–December.

CAUTION: Math required! I promise this is very easy math, *so stick with me.*

Now what we want to do is determine what level of return we want for the property. So if we want a 10% return on our property, we can take the NOI and divide it by our return to get a value.

If we know how much NOI a property has, and we know how much return we want from that property, we have a very easy math equation to figure out what the value of that property is.

All we have to do is divide our income by the return we want, and we will come up with how much we should pay for the property.

So let's say we want a 10% return on our money. We just have to divide the NOI by the return we want to get the value.

Value = $\dfrac{\$60,000}{10\%}$

The value of this property would be… $600,000!

This makes sense because we want to get 10% return on the property, and the property makes $60,000 in NOI a year.

$60,000 is 10% of $600,000.

Seems pretty simple, right? Well, I wish it was that easy.

Unfortunately we do not get to decide what return we want to get and value the property that way.

How it really works is like this: a property type is assigned a level of risk by the market. For example, the market could say that apartment complexes are lower risk than office space. The market could be saying this for whatever reason. The market could say this because more people want to live in apartments and work from home, causing there to be more apartment rental customers than office space renters.

When we reference "the market" we are talking about what is happening between buyers and sellers in transactions. It is the collective price that buyers are willing to pay for something and sellers are willing to sell for.

So, just like the example between Warren and you, the lower risk option is going to be rewarded. For this example, let's say the market tells us the office space is worthy of a 10% return, and because the apartments are less risky, they only need to have a 5% return.

If this NOI belonged to office space:

Value = $\frac{\$60,000}{10\%}$ = $600,000

If this NOI belonged to an apartment:

Value = $\frac{\$60,000}{5\%}$ = $1,200,000

While the properties have the same NOI, they have different values. This is because of the risk associated with one investment over another.

That may seem like a typo to you, but it isn't. If you have ever heard anyone talk about multiplying money, this is what they are referring to. It is very powerful!

CHAPTER 32

CAP RATE

You see, the % we are dividing the NOI by has a name. This is called the "Capitalization Rate" or for short "Cap Rate". The cap rate is extremely powerful and it is how you can make a large amount of money in commercial real estate. You need to remember the cap rate and what it is. It is one of the most important factors in all of real estate.

When you are selling a property, a low cap rate is good because you are going to get a higher price for every dollar of NOI.

If you are buying a property, you generally want a higher cap rate because that means you are getting a good deal, but this rule is not hard and fast. Sometimes an extremely high cap rate can mean something is wrong with the property and you may not want to own it.

Low cap rate = Lower Risk = Every dollar of NOI is more valuable

High cap rate = Higher Risk = Every dollar of NOI is less valuable

Look at the chart below to see what a property with a $60,000 annual NOI could be worth depending on the cap rate used. The property produces the same Net Operating Income, but can have a wide range of possible values.

So the same property can bring in a wide range of sales prices if it were to be sold.

Income	$100,000
Expenses	$40,000
NOI	$60,000
	Value:
10% Cap Rate	$600,000
9% Cap Rate	$666,667
8% Cap Rate	$750,000
7% Cap Rate	$857,143
6% Cap Rate	$1,000,000
5% Cap Rate	$1,200,000
4% Cap Rate	$1,500,000
3% Cap Rate	$2,000,000

You can do these calculations on your own. Pull out your calculator and divide $60,000 by each percentage to see the result for yourself.

Notice how the value of the property between a 10% cap and a 9% cap is smaller than the difference between a 5% cap and a 4% cap. From a 10% cap to a 9% cap, the difference is only $66,667, but from a 5% cap to a 4% cap, there is a $300,000 difference.

It is very important to know the power of the cap rate. If you are buying a property, and the market cap rate is 5%, but the seller tells you they want to sell at a 4% cap rate, the difference does not sound that big. To an untrained ear, they are only asking a 1% difference, "What's the big deal, it's only 1%?"

But in reality, the difference can be huge in how much you pay for a property, or get paid for a property.

The cap rate tells us what % of the purchase price the NOI is going to be over a 12 month period. The cap rate can go up or down depending on the following factors that determine risk:

- Location of property
- Type of property
- Age of property
- Property class
- Real estate market and cycle
- Demand for that property type

Pro Tip: Commercial property brokers know how to weed out newbies to the investing game by only posting a cap rate and an NOI on a property they have for sale. That way if someone calls and asks about the property, and asks what the sales price is, the broker will know the person they are talking with has never bought a piece of property before, and is likely wasting their time. Any seasoned investor should know that with the cap rate and NOI you can determine the purchase price. You will not be taken seriously as a buyer if you make this mistake.

CHAPTER 33

DETERMINING YOUR CAP RATE

Knowing that cap rates are valuable, it is important to know how cap rates are determined. Let's talk about how and why cap rates vary.

LOCATION:

Generally, if we have an apartment complex in Manhattan and the same apartment complex in Alaska, the Alaska apartment is going to be riskier, so the cap rate is going to be higher. Less people living in Alaska means there are fewer potential tenants and that makes it riskier. Higher risk equals higher needed return, so we use a higher cap rate. There are many other factors such as growth, jobs, future expectations, and quality of living that play into the location and how that determines an area's cap rate. The location of your property is a big factor on what cap rate is used.

TYPE:

Property type goes back to my example of apartments vs office space. What kind of property it is will play a factor into the cap rate used. If we see a trend from employees going into offices for work to being able to work at home, that means that businesses will stop renting office spaces now because they are no longer needed. With less potential renters in the market, that office space will become higher risk because of income uncertainty. When there are fewer people who want your office space, it will become more risky.

Same goes for retail space. With so much shopping done online these days, we have seen more purchases done on the internet and less people going into stores to complete a purchase. If people stop buying in stores and only buy online, we will not need stores anymore. This will make storefront real estate less valuable and more risky as an investment.

AGE:

Older properties will in general have higher cap rates than new properties. This is because older properties are higher risk than newer ones. Older properties have functional obsolescence, and higher probability of needing physical repair.

A new property is going to have a new roof, and does not present a risk of needing the roof replaced during ownership. So when we buy older properties, they carry a greater risk of repairs needed. This means more money being spent during ownership and will result in a higher cap rate than their new counterparts.

PROPERTY CLASS:

Ever been in an area where you wouldn't let your mom walk by herself at night? Yea, that's a D or C class area. Ever been to Las Vegas and walked down the strip or in Times Square in New York? That's an A class area.

In real estate, we rank from A to D, with A being most desirable and D being least desirable. An A class property will have a lower cap rate because it is lower risk, and a D class property will have a higher cap rate because it is higher risk.

When comparing, in general, the people who are going to rent from you in a D class area are more likely to damage and not care for your property than an A class area, leading to more unexpected repair costs and therefore risk.

RE MARKET:

This compares the real estate market in 2018 to the real estate market in 2008. In 2008, properties that were selling for 10 caps were selling for 5 caps in 2018. As real estate markets cycle from low demand to high demand, the values are going to change whether the NOI changes or not.

There are many reasons for real estate cycles, but the general rule of thumb is how good the economy is, both in the United States and globally. The better the economy does, the more money the citizens and businesses are going to have, and the more money they will have to buy real estate.

Having money and the ability to buy things is called liquidity, and liquidity is very important in real estate. If nobody has liquidity, then they cannot buy real estate and this is going to hurt prices.

When investors do have liquidity, they are more likely to buy real estate and that is good for prices. The more buyers in the market, the higher the price. The fewer buyers in the market, the lower the price. This is basic supply and demand.

INTEREST RATES:

Interest rates are set by the Federal Reserve (aka the Fed) in America. This is not a government entity, although they work very closely with the government. When things are going poorly in the economy, the federal reserve will typically lower interest rates. This lowers the cost of money for everyone, and allows businesses to get cheaper money.

If they have cheaper money, it means they can borrow more money to invest in their business for less in interest payments. So when business growth slows or comes to stop, the fed lowers interest rates for the whole country. Because banks get their money from the Fed, when the Fed lowers interest rates they can pass those lower rates along to us as investors. Well, when interest rates go down, cap rates go down too. There is generally a spread between interest rates and cap rates. For example, if interest rates are at 5% then cap rates will typically be slightly higher at say 7%. Now if interest rates drop to 4%, then cap rates will start to slide to 6% as more buyers are looking to use lower interest rates to purchase properties. This is an advanced topic, but is worth learning about.

CHAPTER 34

POWER OF THE CAP RATE

L et me give you a quick example of how powerful the cap rate is. At an apartment complex I lived at in Atlanta, the owners implemented a policy where they would take your trash out for you. It was a service where they would come around every night and pick the trash up outside your door and take it to the dumpster for you. This was a mandatory policy they implemented, and it cost an extra $25 a month. Less than a dollar a day for each tenant.

While this doesn't seem like a whole lot of money, there are 196 units at that complex. So the extra income the apartment brings in is going to be 196 x $25 x 12 months = $58,800 a year. But let's say the owner of the apartment had to hire someone to do the labor every night, and this labor takes 2 hours a day at $20 an hour. That's $40 a day x 365 days = $14,600 a year.

Income:	$ 58,800
Expenses:	$-14,600
NOI:	$ 44,200

The owner has added $44,200 extra to their NOI. Let's say the market for these types of apartments is around 6% cap rate. How much did the owner add to the value of their property?

$$\frac{\$44,200}{6\%} = \$???,???$$

While $25 a month doesn't look like much to a single tenant, by implementing this program, the owner of the apartment made $736,667!!!

The value of the property goes up by $736,667 after the first month of implementing this policy at the apartment complex, and the owner of the complex will be able to put that extra cash in his pocket if he were to sell the property.

I hope you are getting this, it is so powerful and this is how fortunes are made in real estate.

Now, if the owner didn't sell the property and he decided to keep it, he would still enjoy an extra $44,200 in cash flow every year, or $3,683 a month.

Now you know how to value commercial real estate! To further your knowledge it will be very helpful for you to actually work through a couple of examples on how to do this yourself. I created three examples with an answer key you can download for free at HaydenCrabtree.com/resources. Also in that download I will give you a google sheet template that will help you out with the math.

TAX BENEFITS

When most people turn the page to a chapter called tax benefits, they most likely yawn and put the book back on the shelf, or skip the chapter entirely.

But you are going to continue reading because you are going to learn how that $736,667 of profit the owner made in the last section can be completely tax free!

Sound good? Sound worthwhile? Alright stick with me because this section, like the last, will change your life.

CHAPTER 35

WHY REAL ESTATE INVESTORS GET TAX BENEFITS

There are 4 main tax benefits that come as a side effect of real estate that can change your financial life. But before we get into the nitty gritty, let's first understand the why.

Why do real estate owners get tax benefits?

It seems like real estate is already juicy enough that people would be interested in investing in it and owning it, that we really don't need the icing on the cake. Well, that's probably true, but the government has decided that it wants to make sure we are interested. They want to be sure that our spare money goes into real estate investing instead of other places we could put our money.

The government also wants to be sure that we buy U.S. real estate to stimulate our economy rather than real estate in Europe, South America, or somewhere else so they give us great benefits.

You see, the government puts out a playbook that guides our taxes called the tax code. Now some people see the tax code and look at all the ways the government is trying to take your money away from you. But when real estate investors look at the tax code, they look at it as a playbook, an instruction manual.

The government puts out the tax code and gives incentives for things they want to happen. If the government wants us to buy a house, they give an incentive where you can deduct your interest expense on homes from your taxable income.

If they want us to donate to charity, they give us a tax break there too. The 4 main parts of the big tax breaks for real estate are incentives the government gives us, because they want us to provide real estate space for rent.

If you try and fight the tax code, you will lose. If you make the tax code your friend, you will win.

Some people think that paying taxes is their patriotic duty. The opposite is true! If you are paying taxes, that means you are not doing what your government wants you to do to help the nation.

Paying taxes is a penalty. Paying no taxes should be our goal. Yes, it is possible to pay no taxes at all. In fact, I know many people making millions a year and paying zero in taxes annually.

None. Zero.

The same can be true for you.

The truth is, NOT paying taxes is more patriotic than paying taxes because you are helping your government out by giving its citizens apartments to rent, storage units to store in, office space to work in, medical space for doctors to use, or grocery stores to shop in. The government wants to cut you a tax break, so let's learn how we can make our government happy!

CHAPTER 36

DEPRECIATION IS YOUR FRIEND

What most people think of is not the kind of depreciation we are talking about. We are not talking about what happens to a new car's value when you drive it off the lot for the first time. That is bad depreciation. We want good depreciation.

As mentioned earlier, when you buy an investment property, the IRS is going to recognize that that building is going to break down a little bit each and every year.

The slow deterioration over time of a building is why we are awarded depreciation.

The IRS tells us that buildings that people are going to live in will go from full value to $0 over 27.5 years. They tell us properties that people do not live in will go down over 39 years. The following chart will show us how much we can write off every year on a $1,000,000 building.

Looking at this chart for both residential and commercial properties, we can see how much we get to "depreciate". We bought the properties for $1,000,000. For the residential property, we get to take $1,000,000 and divide it by 27.5. This will give us $36,364 we get to take as an expense each year.

$1,000,000 Purchase				
Year	Residential (27.5)	Basis	Commercial (39)	Basis
1	$36,364	$963,636	$25,641	$974,359

For commercial, we take the same $1,000,000 and divide it by 39, to get $25,641 as an expense each year.

The numbers in the "basis" column represent the original purchase price, minus the depreciation. This is called the basis, and it is a way to see how much more we will get to take as depreciation expense in the future.

To calculate the basis for the residential at the end of year 1, we take $1,000,000 - $36,364 = $963,636

To calculate the basis for the commercial we take $1,000,000 - $25,641 = $974,359.

Looking at the next chart for year 2, you will see we take the same $36,364 for residential and $25,641 for commercial. The basis at the end of year 2 will be the basis at the end of year 1 minus how much we took in year 2.

$1,000,000 Purchase				
Year	Residential (27.5)	Basis	Commercial (39)	Basis
1	$36,364	$963,636	$25,641	$974,359
2	$36,364	$927,273	$25,641	$948,718

The following chart shows how a basis goes down over a 10 year time frame.

		$1,000,000 Purchase		
Year	Residential (27.5)	Basis	Commercial (39)	Basis
1	$36,364	$963,636	$25,641	$974,359
2	$36,364	$927,273	$25,641	$948,718
3	$36,364	$890,909	$25,641	$923,077
4	$36,364	$854,545	$25,641	$897,436
5	$36,364	$818,182	$25,641	$871,795
6	$36,364	$781,818	$25,641	$846,154
7	$36,364	$745,455	$25,641	$820,513
8	$36,364	$709,091	$25,641	$794,872
9	$36,364	$672,727	$25,641	$769,231
10	$36,364	$636,364	$25,641	$743,590

For the residential property, we took a total of $363,640 of depreciation. This means that over that 10 year time period we could have made $363,640 and not had to pay any taxes on it.

For the commercial property, we took a total of $256,410 of depreciation. This means that over that 10 year time period we could have made $256,410 and not had to pay any taxes on it.

On a $1,000,000 building that people use as homes (dwelling or what I am referring to above as residential), we get to take $36,364 each year as an expense.

But did we really pay that $36,364 to anyone? The answer is no!

Because the government wants us to own these buildings, they allow us to take this expense. The amount we would get taxed on for the investment from the previous chapter would look like this:

Dwelling purchased for $1,000,000:
(NOI) $60,000 - (Depreciation) $36,364 = $23,636 Taxable amount

OR

Income	$100,000
Expense	$ -40,000
NOI	$ 60,000
Depreciation	$ -36,364
Taxable amount	$ 23,636

Commercial purchased for $1,000,000:

(NOI) $60,000 - (Depreciation) $25,641 = $34,359 Taxable amount

Income	$100,000
Expense	$ -40,000
NOI	$ 60,000
Depreciation	$ -25,641
Taxable amount	$ 34,359

To make this clear, the depreciation is not an actual expense. We pay no money for depreciation.

Isn't that great! We get to take the full depreciation amount out each year as if we had spent that money, when really we didn't! That is tax free cash straight in our pocket!

If this sounds awesome, wait for the next section on cost segregation.

As you can see, the government wants us to invest in housing (dwelling) more than other assets. The government is more worried about its citizens having housing than it is other space, so they give us bigger tax breaks on dwellings so we as investors will focus our attention there.

Before we move on, notice the column labeled "basis". This is the amount left in a property at the end of each year that you can depreciate. This is important to know, because once that basis reaches $0, you run out of depreciation. As you can see on the chart above, you calculate your basis by subtracting your previous year basis minus how much depreciation you used this year.

It is also worth noting that when you buy a property, the government will only let you depreciate the buildings. You can not depreciate land. When you buy a property, you will have to split the purchase price up between how much of the purchase price was for the land and how much was for the buildings, which are also known as "improvements."

CHAPTER 37

DEPRECIATION STEROIDS

This is where the tax benefits get juicy, so grab a highlighter.

Building off of what we just learned about depreciation, the government wanted to make it even sweeter for us investors! Now this is actually a pro tip, as I talk to many investors who have never heard about this strategy. It is called accelerated depreciation which is done through a cost segregation study.

Here is the general logic behind this: the government will let us depreciate a dwelling over 27.5 years. But realistically, not everything in the building deteriorates at the same pace. You see, a roof is going to last you 15 years, but the floors are only going to last 5 years. The walls are only going to last 4 years, and the foundation is going to last 40. You get the point, not everything breaks down at the same pace.

So what we are allowed to do is hire a professional to do a cost segregation study on our property. In this study they go through and look at each individual component of a building. They look at the concrete, the wood in the walls, the wires running to the lights, the pipes to the sink, the shower tiles. Then, they depreciate each of those at their own pace.

It may say that wood is going to last 3 years, so let's take that value of that wood, and instead of breaking it out over 27.5 years, let's break it out over 3 years.

It may also say that electrical wiring is going to last 5 years, so instead of waiting 27.5 years, let's break out and depreciate the value of the wire over 5 years.

This is really just a tax game that we are playing. Even if we depreciate wood in 3 years and our wires in 5 years, we really expect for those items to be working fine in 3 or 5 years. We simply want to get as much depreciation as we possibly can.

What this does is it takes a large bulk of your depreciation and moves it into the first couple of years. This is a huge benefit! This study does have to be done by a professional, but is worth the cost. You can find a pro by googling "cost segregation study real estate."

I personally have seen up to 40% of the purchase price written off in year 1 as an expense.

From the example in the previous section: taking 40% of a $1,000,000 piece of property.

(NOI) $60,000 - (Accelerated Depreciation) $400,000 = $ -340,000 Taxable amount

OR

Income	$ 100,000
Expense	$ -40,000
NOI	$ 60,000
Depreciation	$ -400,000
Taxable amount	$ -340,000

Yes, you are reading that right. We are going to show a $340,000 dollar loss from this property in year 1.

Did we lose $340,000? The answer is no!

We had a positive cash flow, but the government is going to recognize us as having lost money on the project this year. So if you are a doctor or an engineer, guess what? You get to take this "loss" and move it over to your personal tax returns. From there, you will get to subtract this off of your personal taxes, shielding your other income from taxes too!

So if a doctor makes $500,000 from their practice, they will get to write off $360,000. What you will pay taxes on will look like the following:

Income from being a DR.	$ 500,000
Loss from real estate investment	$(360,000)
Income taxable	$ 140,000

Yes, this doctor will still pay taxes on $140,000, but look at how much money he just saved. He was going to have to pay around $211,000 in taxes without depreciation. Now he is only going to have to pay $45k in taxes. He saved $166,000 in taxes in the first year!!!!!

Using a bank, he would have only spent $200k of his own money to buy this $1,000,000 property. He almost makes that entire amount back in the first year from *tax savings alone!* Not to mention the cash flow from the property.

In addition to that, he gets his equity build up, appreciation and cash flow all occurring at the same time. Major wealth is being built!

What if you are an engineer that made $70,000, what will your taxes look like?

Income from being an engineer	$ 70,000
Loss from real estate investment	$(360,000)
Income taxable	$(290,000)

You pay no taxes! In addition to that, you get to take your $290,000 loss and roll it forward to next year. Your "losses" get to roll forward and protect next year's income as well! Losses get to carry forward each year, so you are not hurting your future self by taking as much depreciation as possible up front.

Oh yeah, and everytime you fix your building up, you get to reset the depreciation clock on that component of your building, resulting in more depreciation.

Do you understand the power of accelerated depreciation? Let's all be good citizens and buy some properties for the government so we don't have to pay taxes!

Does this sound too good to be true or illegal? Tax fraud maybe? I beg you to call a qualified CPA and confirm all this today. Like, right now! Do it!

CHAPTER 38

TAX FREE PROPERTY SWAP

Some of you will not believe the content that is in this section. When we are talking about building up your real estate snowball, this could be the #1 source of fuel on the fire.

What we are talking about here is a 1031 exchange.

Here is the concept. When we buy a property for $1,000,000 and sell it for $1,500,000 10 years later, we have $500,000 of gain from the original purchase price. But over those 5 years, we also took a massive amount of depreciation to shield our income, so let's say our basis is at only $100,000. So if we sell this property we have to pay taxes on the difference between the sales proceeds and the current basis. So we would have to pay taxes on $1,400,000 gain.

ZOINKS!

Not good, and at this point it makes depreciation sound less enticing. This is where the 1031 exchange comes into play.

The 1031 exchange allows you to take those sales proceeds and buy another property with that money. As long as you buy a property with your sales proceeds, you do not have to pay any taxes on the gains.

Yes, that's right, *no taxes on your gains.*

So the apartment owner who implemented the trash program that made himself an extra $736,667 could take that profit and he could move it forward, tax free. He does not have to use any of his depreciation to shield this either. You can have depreciation AND 1031. They are a great combination that can help you avoid taxes for the rest of your life. It is an awesome program if used correctly.

Let's say you buy a house for $100,000 and you use a low money down program. You put down 5% ($5,000). This house is a fixer-upper and you think that after you do some work to it, live in it for a year, rent it out for a year, then you can sell it for $200,000.

When you sell it for $200,000, you will owe the bank $90,000. So you will walk away with $200,000 - $90,000 = $110,000. Out of this $110,000, you have around a $100,000 gain which is taxable.

Sounds pretty sweet! You could take the money and run, but you would have to pay taxes on that $100,000 gain. Depending on your personal situation, how much you pay in taxes could vary but let's say it's going to be 20% or $20,000.

You could pay your $20,000 in taxes or what you could do is 1031 that money into small commercial property that would cost $500,000. You would have to put 20% down on a commercial property. It works out perfect because you have $110,000 in your 1031 exchange you can use to buy a new property tax free.

You now buy that commercial property, use it for cash flow and depreciation. Fix it up and raise the income to get the NOI up. Now let's say you sell it after 2 years and it is worth $800,000. Your original loan from the bank was $400,000, so by now it is down to $380,000 because it went down from your monthly payments.

So from this sale you walk away with $800,000 - $380,000 = $420,000. Now, you could take the money and run, but you are going to have a huge tax bill. You have a gain on the property of $800,000 - $500,000 = $300,000.

In addition to this, you have also depreciated the property, so your taxable base is going to be well over $300,000. This would result in paying over $60,000 in taxes at a 20% rate.

Some people will look at it and realize they turned $5,000 into over $200,000 after taxes and be very happy with that.

Then there are those who realize with $420,000 in tax free 1031 money they could buy a $2,100,000 property.

The cash flow from that property should be in the neighborhood of $50,000 a year.

If you wanted to continue this playbook you could have over $1,000,000 of 1031 money in the next step up the ladder. At this point you can buy properties close to $5,000,000 and the cash flow could exceed $100,000 a year. Or you could keep your $2,100,000 property and enjoy the cash flow from it as inflation happens and your debt is paid down by your tenants. Not bad considering you started with only $5k at the beginning of this story.

The 1031 exchange is extremely powerful when utilized correctly. There are some drawbacks that you should be aware of. The first drawback is that when you sell your property you have 45 days to identify a replacement property and 180 days to actually buy the property you say you are going to. This is OK if you already know which property you are going to buy. But, it can lead to making poor decisions because you are trying to avoid paying taxes.

It also puts you in a very weak negotiating position if the seller of a property you are trying to buy knows you are in a 1031 exchange, because that tells them you are working on a limited timeline.

The next drawback is that you can only identify 3 potential properties. If you identify more, you have to buy them all or pay your taxes. The purchase price of the properties you buy has to be more than the sales price of the property you sold too. You always have to buy a bigger and bigger property.

CHAPTER 39

REFI TIL YOU DIE

While 1031 exchanges sound like and are powerful builders of wealth, there is another tool in the investor toolbox that is just as powerful, and you have already heard about it.

The banks are willing to give us a % of what the property is worth in the form of a loan when we buy the property. In commercial the maximum you are generally going to see a maximumof 80% of the purchase price funded by a bank in the form of a loan. This is what the money split will look like when we first buy the property:

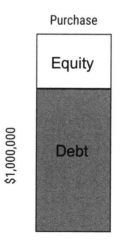

The total height of this bar represents the entire value of the property. The shaded part of the bar is debt, or what the bank gave us to buy the property. The clear part of the bar is the money we had to put in, also called equity.

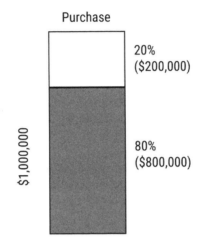

The $200,000 is called equity and the $800,000 is called debt. You currently have $200,000 in equity in the property. A formula you should know, because it is fundamental in real estate, business and personal wealth is this:

Assets = Debts + Equity

In the above chart we have as much debt on the property as a bank will give us. We are "fully leveraged" on this particular property.

Now, let's say that you have owned this property for 5 years, and your property value has increased to $1,200,000 due to inflation. Your debt is now down to $700,000 because you have been paying it off. Let's plug in our numbers to the above equation. The property is the asset. What you owe the bank is your debt.

$$\begin{aligned} \text{Assets} \quad &= \quad \text{Debts} \; + \text{Equity} \\ \$1{,}200{,}000 &= \$700{,}000 + \text{Equity} \end{aligned}$$

5 years after purchase

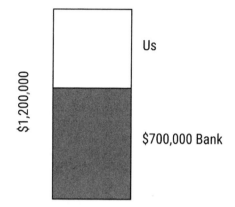

So we have our asset value and we have our debt value. We can figure out our equity value.

$$\$1,200,000 - \$700,000 = \text{Equity}$$

What is our equity value? That's right, it is now $500,000.

$$\$1,200,000 - \$700,000 = \$500,000$$

5 years after purchase

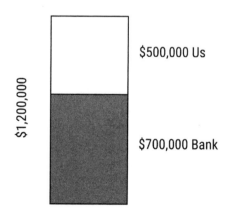

Yes, you now have $500,000!

Notice what happened here? You started off with $200,000 in equity. Because the loan got paid down you made $100,000 in equity. You made another $200,000 in equity because the property value went from $1,000,000 to $1,200,000. In total you turned $200,000 into $500,000.

Because banks are in the business of lending money, they will also give us a loan on properties we own that have extra equity in them. Yes, that is right, a bank will give you a loan on a property you own. You do not have to sell a property in order to get the extra equity out of them.

So in the above situation we have a property that is worth $1,200,000. The bank is still willing to give us 80% of whatever the property is worth. 80% x $1,200,000 = $960,000.

If we take the bank up on this, we have to pay off our current loan. The current loan with the bank is $700,000. To calculate what we would end up with, we would subtract the old loan from the new loan.

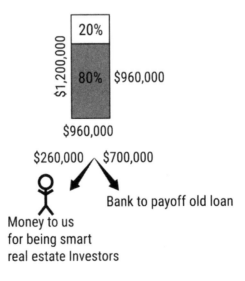

New Loan = 80% x property value
New Loan = 80% x $1,200,000
New Loan = $960,000

Money to us = New Loan - Old Loan
Money to us = $960,000 - $700,000
Money to us = $260,000

At the end of this exercise, we are going to have $260,000 left over that is going to come to us. The best part about this $260k?

It is all tax free. No taxes are paid on this money.

"Wait a second!" You are thinking. "It's tax free… Does that mean there are limits to what I can spend that money on? Can I only use it to buy other real estate like a 1031?"

NOPE! You can use this money for whatever you want. Take a vacation, go on a shopping spree, buy yourself a Lamborghini if you want!

This money is yours and you can do whatever you want with it. This process is called a refinance or "refi" for slang. Specifically what we are doing is a "cash out refi" because you are getting your cash out.

Now, if you are a *savvy investor* you will realize that using this money to *buy more cash flow* real estate is a smart play, but I am not going to tell you how to live your life.

The money comes out tax free because it is technically debt. The money will have to be repaid to the bank at some point. But you already know and understand this. *You aren't paying for this debt, your tenants are.* As a general rule, when you refi, your loan payments will go up.

Let's look at the property before the refi.

Before refi

Income	$100,000
Expense	$ -40,000
NOI	$ 60,000
Debt Service	$ -15,000
Cash flow	$ 45,000

You have a $60,000 NOI, with $15,000 of debt payments. This makes your cash flow $45,000.

Now let's take a look at what happens to the numbers after our refi.

After Refi

Income	$100,000
Expense	$ -40,000
NOI	$ 60,000
Debt Service	$ -25,000
Cash flow	$ 35,000

Your NOI is still $60,000, but your debt payments have gone from $15,000 to $25,000. This drops your cash flow from $45,000 to $35,000.

By taking a cash out refi you are exchanging money now for money later. You are taking a lump sum now, and increasing your payments in the future. Your monthly cash flow is going to go down because your loan amount with the bank increased, therefore increasing your monthly payment.

Loan Amount ↑ = Debt Service ↑

A great way to think about this money is an advance from your property. How long would it take your property to pay you the refi proceeds? In the equation above, we increased our annual debt payments by $10,000 (from 15k to 25k) and we got to take out $290,000 in cash. So it would have taken us $290,000 / $10,000 = 29 years to save this much cash in the form of cash flow from the property.

We essentially gave ourselves a financial shortcut of 29 years. Pretty awesome! I love little financial hacks like this, especially when they are tax free.

Again, call your CPA and confirm this information for yourself if it sounds too good to be true!

(please note the above is just an example and not real world numbers. We are going to get into real world numbers in the next section on debt)

CHAPTER 40

INTEREST WRITE OFF

To come back around to the point that the government and IRS wants us to borrow money, they have written in the tax code that you get to take the interest on a loan as an expense for operating your piece of real estate. We will dive into how it is determined how much of a loan payment is interest and how much is going to repaying the actual debt in the next chapter, but for now let's use a ballpark figure. On the above amount of $25,000 of debt payments to the bank each year, you are going to have say $20,000 of interest payments.

Taxable amount if you did not use debt:

Income	$ 100,000
Expense	$ -40,000
NOI	$ 60,000
Depreciation	$-400,000
Taxable amount	$-360,000

Taxable amount if you did use debt:

Income	$ 100,000
Expense	$ -40,000
NOI	$ 60,000
Depreciation	$-400,000
Interest payment	$ -20,000
Taxable amount	$-380,000

So by using debt to own this property, we get an extra tax benefit of being able to write off the interest we pay as an expense to the property. This is another benefit of using debt over not using debt to purchase a property. The government is rewarding you for borrowing money!

If you make a lot of money and have a huge tax bill, there is another powerful tool called conservation easements that you can use. That is a topic that is too advanced for the pages of this book, but if you would like to learn more about this you can google it or talk to a knowledgeable CPA.

ROI check in—are you getting value out of this book?

Has this book changed your life, or at least given you the information you can use to change your life? If the answer is yes, then *please do me a favor and text someone you care about this link:* HaydenCrabtree.com/freebook and I will send them this same book for free.

Send it to someone who has a growth mindset like you! Please do not keep all this goodness for yourself. Let's spread the love around! And plus if the other person gets the book you will have someone you can discuss all of this with and hold each other accountable to making real world progress.

DEBT

OVERVIEW

Reading through and understanding this section in full will put you so far ahead of the rest of the world in terms of financial education. We are going to talk about how a payment is determined, interest rates, types of debt, the "landmines" of debt, and where most people go wrong.

As we have already talked about, a bank will lend you money to buy a property. In return, you will pay the bank a set amount over a certain number of years as repayment for that money. But banks do not do this for free, they want some interest on their money, and that is how banks make a profit.

DEFINITIONS:

Balance – How much you owe the bank if you were to pay it off now

Payment – Also called a mortgage payment, or debt service. It is the amount you pay to the bank each month.

Principal – Money that goes towards paying off the loan each payment

Interest – Money that the bank keeps as profit in each payment

Amortization – How long will it take you to pay off the loan

Points – The up front fee for the loan

Balloon – When is the loan amount due?

LTV – Loan to Value. Simply saying what % of the property value will the bank give us as debt.

CHAPTER 41

HOW A LOAN WORKS

The biggest misconception that most people have when it comes to debt is thinking that it is paid off in a straight line. That every payment has the same amount go towards paying off the loan as goes towards interest. They think that if they owe the bank $100,000 and make a $1,000 payment each month, that they are paying $500 of interest and $500 in principal each month. From there they think that after one month, the amount they will owe the bank will be $99,500.

Most people think loan repayment looks like this:

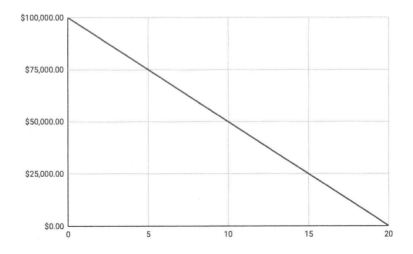

Most people think that the amount you owe the bank goes down in a straight line.

This is not the case. The truth is that no 2 payments are exactly the same. You see, we are going to pay the bank a different split each time we make a payment. The bank is going to make sure that they get their interest before you actually start to pay down the loan.

So in the beginning you are going to pay a huge amount of interest, and a small amount of principal. On a $1,000 payment, $900 of it may be interest, and only $100 principal. This means if you had a balance of $100,000, after that first payment of $1,000, you are going to have a balance of $99,900.

Payment	Payment amount	Interest	Principal	Balance	Balance decrease
0	$0	$0	$0	$100,000	
1	$1,000	$900	$100	$99,900	-$100

Every month, you are going to start paying more and more towards the principal. Because you now owe less than $100,000 to the bank, you are going to pay less interest. The next payment may look something like this: $1,000 payment, $899 interest, $101 principal.

Now your balance goes from $99,900 to $99,799. The amount you owe over time is going look something like this:

Notice in this chart how the total payment is the same, but there is a difference in how much of that payment went to interest and how much of it went to principal.

Payment	Payment amount	Interest	Principal	Balance	Balance decrease
0	$0	$0	$0	$100,000	
1	$1,000	$900	$100	$99,900	-$100
2	$1,000	$899	$101	$99,799	-$101

Total Payment = Interest payment + Principal Payment

As the interest payment goes down, the principal payment goes up and the total payment stays the same.

Over the first 12 payments it would looks like this:

Payment	Payment amount	Interest	Principal	Balance	Balance decrease
0	$0	$0	$0	$100,000	
1	$1,000	$900	$100	$99,900	-$100
2	$1,000	$899	$101	$99,799	-$101
3	$1,000	$898	$102	$99,697	-$102
4	$1,000	$897	$103	$99,594	-$103
5	$1,000	$896	$104	$99,490	-$104
6	$1,000	$895	$105	$99,385	-$105
7	$1,000	$894	$106	$99,279	-$106
8	$1,000	$893	$107	$99,172	-$107
9	$1,000	$892	$108	$99,064	-$108
10	$1,000	$891	$109	$98,955	-$109
11	$1,000	$890	$110	$98,845	-$110
12	$1,000	$889	$111	$98,734	-$111

At payment 0, we have made no payment yet, so we still owe $100,000. Look in the "balance" column for the amount we still owe the bank. While our payment amount stays the exact same, we are paying a different amount of interest and principal with each payment. To get the balance after a payment, you will subtract this payment's principal split from the previous balance.

In the first couple of payments, we are paying a huge amount of interest. A large majority of that money is not going towards reducing our balance. Another way to put this is we are not reducing the amount we owe the bank by very much, instead much of our payment is profit for the bank.

With each month, more and more of our payment is going towards actually paying down the loan. Most people do not understand this. Please study the above chart to get this concept embedded in your brain.

This trend will continue all the way until the loan is paid off. Your first payment will be $1,000 (with $900 going towards interest and $100 going to principal). Your last payment will also be $1,000 (with $5 going towards interest and $995 going towards principal. The interest that you pay each month is going to be based off of how much principal you have. It looks something like this: interest paid = (interest rate/12) x balance.

Anything left over above the interest you owe goes towards balance reduction. As the balance reduces each month, so does your interest, and the amount you are paying towards principal goes up.

Over the life of the loan the payoff would look like the following chart. Notice how it is not a straight line. Look how much principal is paid down between year 0 and year 5.

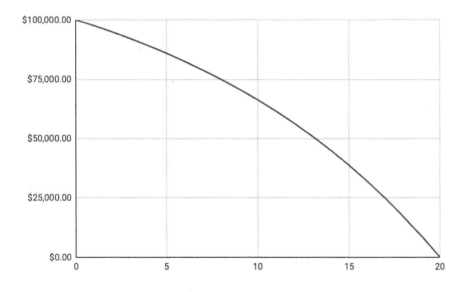

Now compare that amount with how much principal was paid down between year 15 and year 20. Same amount of time, but much more actual debt was paid down.

In the real world numbers do not round out evenly and they do not go down in a straight line. To go further in depth in a free video and grab a spreadsheet that will show you how debt actually gets paid down with real numbers, go to HaydenCrabtree.com/resources

CHAPTER 42

INTEREST RATES

Interest rates are the amount a bank wants to make on their money every year. So if the bank lends you $100,000 and you have a 5% interest rate, they want to make $5,000 of interest. If you have a 6% interest rate, you are going to pay them $6,000 a year. This is the price of money.

The bank will determine what interest rate is appropriate according to what the interest rates are in the market, how risky your project is, and how creditworthy you are. The interest rates in the market are set by the federal reserve, or by the price of government bonds, depending on what your lender likes to use.

There are several different indexes your lender may use. Be sure to ask your lender which index they tie their rates to.

If your project is mining for gold in China, that would be considered a risky venture and would require a high interest rate. If your project was buying well performing apartments in the fastest growing city in America, you could get a low interest rate.

Interest rates will also be impacted by how long you choose to pay your loan off. If you choose for it to take a long time to pay your loan off, the bank is going to want a higher interest rate. If you choose to do it in a shorter amount of time, you are likely to get a lower interest rate. This amount of time you wait to pay off your loan is called amortization.

CHAPTER 43

AMORTIZATION

This is how long it takes you to pay off the loan. We will see amortization rates in terms of years. It can range anywhere from 10 years to 35 years depending on the project. Now if you borrow the same amount of money, $100,000, you could have wildly different monthly payments depending on your amortization rate.

If a loan needs to be paid off in 10 years, your payment is going to be much higher than if it needed to be paid off in 35 years. The 10 year amortization payment at 5% interest will be $1,060 a month. At 35 years to amortize, at the same 5% interest, your monthly payment will be $504. Even though you borrowed the same amount of money, your payment is cut in half!

The duration in which you amortize debt will directly impact your cash flow. *

10 Year amortization cash flow		35 Year amortization cash flow	
Income	$2,000	Income	$2,000
Expense	$ 500	Expense	$ 500
NOI	$1,500	NOI	$1,500
Debt	$1,060	Debt	$ 504
Cash flow	$ 440	Cash flow	$ 996

The same exact property can produce different cash flows depending on what kind of debt you use to buy it. This is a major key to understand.

Different amortizations will often come at different rates, so it is extremely important to fully understand how debt works before you actually borrow any money.

So what amortization rate should you aim for? Should you pay your debt off sooner and have less cash flow or pay it off longer and have more cash flow?

This is an advanced conversation so I made a video to explain my thoughts on this. Watch the video I made explaining this decision here: haydencrabtree. com/resources

CHAPTER 44

BALLOONS

N o, we are not talking about a balloon like a birthday party. But for a visual representation, let's use one.

You have a balloon that is blown up to 100% capacity. Your goal is to get the balloon completely emptied of all air. You begin doing this by very slowly letting air out. At the end of 1 minute you have let 3% of the air out. Now your balloon is at 97% capacity. You do it for another minute and you let 5% more air out. You are now at 92% capacity. You continue to do this at an accelerated rate, and by the end of 10 minutes you are at 0%.

This is how a 10 year amortizing loan works. Every minute is equal to a year, and the amount of air you let out is the amount you are paying towards the balance. Each minute you let out more air than you did the minute before until the balloon is empty. When you reach 0% you have no more debt.

Now we introduce our little sibling who is impatient, let's call him Johnny. Johnny is watching you do this, but after 3 minutes he grows impatient, grabs a needle and pops your balloon, letting all the air out at once.

Johnny is the bank. The bank does not like to wait the full amortization period to get their money back. While we could wait the full 10 minutes to let the air out and get to 0%, the bank thinks they should do it quicker and let all the air out when the balloon still has 70% of its air in it.

When we first take out a loan, the bank is going to tell us what amortization the loan is going to be paid off, and when the money is actually going to be due. I know, doesn't make much sense, but the bank does this because they face a risk called interest rate risk.

If a bank makes a loan for $100,000 at 5% and then in 5 years interest rates have risen to 9%, the bank is shooting themselves in the foot because you have their money, and you have it locked in at 5% even though if you were to go get a new loan, you would have to pay 9%. For us as borrowers, locking in an interest rate is good because we know what we are going to pay. For banks this is bad because they lose the opportunity to charge more in interest.

To combat this risk, banks implement these "balloons" where they tell you that all the money is currently due. Now do you actually have to come up with all the money? For the most part, this is just a procedure the bank implements to reset your interest rates to whatever they are at that time. They will issue you a new loan for the exact same amount that you're going to have to pay them.

This is where things got dicey in 2008. Investors had debt balloons that were coming due in 2009. Well, in 2009 no banks were lending money, even on properties that were doing well. That's because the banks didn't have the money to lend. The majority of these projects were development projects where people who were getting loans that had a balloon 12 months to 24 months after the loan started.

A major key to any real estate investment that you do is to GET LONG TERM DEBT. This means taking balloon payments that are very far away. Many bankers will ask for 3 year balloons. A banker wants a short balloon because it reduces their interest rate risk, and they get paid a fee each time we get a new loan.

As investors we want balloons that are very far away. It is possible to negotiate with banks, and always negotiate the balloon payment as far away from today as possible. It may cost you a little bit of a higher interest rate, but having a balloon further away is a great way to reduce your future risk.

By making your balloon payment very far in the future, you allow yourself options if a crash were to happen. *If a crash happens, you will be fine as long as your tenants keep paying rent and your debt is not due.* If your tenants keep paying, they will cover your expenses, pay your mortgage, and put cash flow in your pocket.

Please realize that you could do nothing wrong and your property could be performing well, but if you have a balloon due and you can't pay for it because banks aren't lending, you may have to sell the property well below what it is worth or give the property back to the bank. This is why it is important to buy stable cash flow properties and get long term debt.

You can tell your banker that you are willing to pay a little higher interest rate now in order for your balloon period to be pushed back further into the future. Your payments may be slightly higher, but you are going to reduce your risk, which is what investing is all about.

They are also less common, but loans do exist where there is no balloon due ever. Your loan will never be due and your only obligation is to pay the mortgage each month for the full amortization period. This is called a "fully amortizing loan."

CHAPTER 45

TYPES OF LOANS

There are a few types of loans you should know about. The first is a traditional loan like we have explained above. This is the most common and is what you will deal with a majority of the time.

The next loan type is called interest only. Exactly like it sounds, on this loan you only pay interest. If we had a 5% interest rate and borrowed $100,000, then our payments would be exactly $5,000 a year, or $416 a month. When this loan came due, we would have to pay back exactly the same amount we originally borrowed, $100,000.

So if we borrowed the $100k as above for 5 years, we would make $416 payments every month, and then in 60 months we would have to pay back the full $100k. These loans are less common, and are harder to find. The benefit is that you boost your cash flow because you are not paying the principal down. The downfall is that you are not benefiting from any equity build up over time.

The next loan type is called variable rate. As it sounds, this is where your interest rate changes as interest rates in the market change. Your rate will be tied to some type of index and will change at some preset time period, like every quarter. So if your rate was tied to the fed fund rate, and was set at the fed fund rate + 2%, your interest rate would track that rate, which is set by the fed, plus 2%.

So if the fed fund rate went down, your interest rate would go down without having to get a new loan. You would also have to pay a higher rate if the rates in the market go up, so this type of loan provides uncertainty as to what your payment will be in the future.

Now that you understand more about how debt works, you can understand where some of the risks of real estate investing lie. You see, in real estate, *success is a combination of the cash flows from a property, the value of the property, as well as how you finance the property.* If you know how to make the value go up but do not finance it properly, you will be less effective.

CHAPTER 46

POINTS

Points are what you pay to the bank as an up front fee. If you borrow $100,000, and you the fee is 1 point, then you are going to have to pay them $1,000 up front to get this loan. If you have to pay them a point and a half, that's a $1,500 fee. 2 points would be $2,000. You get how this works.

These are also called origination fees or bank fees. It is just another way for the bank to make money off of you, and can many times be used as a bonus or commission for the person handling your loan at the bank.

These are negotiable, but think about what I said about a realtor. If you try to squeeze them out of their commission, how hard are they going to fight for you to try and get you the best deal possible?

If you squeeze them, will they want to pick up your call the next time you call for a loan on the next property? If everybody wins...then everybody wins! So don't try and cut someone on their payday if they are helping you make money.

CHAPTER 47

LOAN TO VALUE (LTV)

D ebt, which is also called leverage, can explode your property's financial returns for you as an investor. Loan to value (LTV) is important to understand because it will help us buy, refinance and optimize our real estate investments.

LTV = <u>Loan Amount</u>
       Property Value

The general rule for a commercial investment is that you are going to be able to get up to 80% LTV. That means if we are buying a property for $1,000,000, the bank is going to give us $800,000. If we are buying for $2,000,000, they will give us $1,600,000. We will have come up with the rest of the money to buy the property.

The bank has lines drawn in the sand when it comes to LTV. Why is that? The banks are in the money business. They like to lend money, they do not like to manage and own real estate. To protect themselves from ever having to own and operate property, they build a buffer into the property to make sure that if they ever had to sell it, they could get all their money back.

So if you were to go out and buy this property for $1M with an 80% LTV loan and you failed. The bank has to foreclose on the property. They would want to turn around and get rid of this property as quickly as they could. They are not concerned with getting the maximum amount of money out of this project, instead they just want their money back. So they will sell this property to the first person that comes along and offers them $800,000 for it, which many investors will because it is worth $1M. The bank only wants to get their $800,000 back so they can turn around and lend it again.

The bank likes to build these buffers in so they can recoup their money in the worst case scenario. The banks also like for us to have skin in the game so that we are really paying attention to that property performing well. The banks want us to know that if the investment goes bad, we are losing our money before the bank loses their money.

If this property failed and we sold for $900,000 to avoid being foreclosed on, even though the bank put up 80% and we put up 20%, we would lose $100k and the bank would get repaid in full. We would still walk away with the money left over after the bank gets their money ($900k - $800k = $100k).

Banks have first right to all monies that come out of the property, but they also do not get to share in the upside profits when a project goes well.

There you have it. That is the overview into how debt works and how it can benefit a real estate investor.

Read and reread this section many times. Learn all you can about debt, and how it works.

As mentioned in the beginning of this book, debt is a tool, like a chainsaw. When you know how to handle a chainsaw, you can be very effective at cutting down trees. But, when you do not handle a chainsaw with care, things get ugly.

SECTION 9

UNDERWRITING AN INVESTMENT

CHAPTER 48

ANALYZE THE PROPERTY

This is a crucial chapter to understand before you get into your first investment. *To underwrite means to analyze.* It is a fancy financial word for taking a closer look at the numbers.

When we are underwriting a property, we are going to create a "proforma." The purpose of a proforma is to analyze our income, expenses, NOI, debt service, cash flows, and overall performance for an investment over a period of time.

By looking at a proforma, we should be able to predict with accuracy what our cash flow from a property will be, what the value of a property will be in the future, and what kind of money we can expect to make.

I have analyzed thousands of deals and used all the tools out there that are supposed to help investors analyze potential investments. But they all missed the mark. So, I decided to take matters into my own hands, and I created what I think is the world's best real estate calculator in MyPropertyStats.Com. No matter if you are brand new to investing, or have been in real estate for 20 years, My Property Stats creates world class investment analysis in just minutes. This will help you analyze any real estate deal to know if it has good returns and if you should buy it, or move onto a different property. Even cooler than that, I built the system with a special feature that will tell you exactly the price to pay for any deal.

Also, if you are a real estate Agent or Broker, using My Property Stats can help you make more money by creating amazing proformas to help sell investment properties to investors.

So, if you want to start analyzing deals with more accuracy and less time, go check it out now at MyPropertyStats.com.

Now let's get back to learning.

In the previous chapters, I have shown you a very basic proforma. It goes like this:

> Income
> - Expenses
> = NOI
> - Debt
> = Cash flow

This is a great way to quickly analyze a property, but the truth is that this is too simplistic. This format only looks at one time period, a single year for example, and only analyzes the income statement.

In real estate we have two statements that we need to be aware of. The first is the income statement, the next is the balance sheet. These two statements are equally as important for real estate as they are for your personal financial life and any business.

The income statement (referred to as Profit and Loss or P&L) is where we are going to show income and expenses. This is where we will find our NOI as well as our cash flows.

The balance sheet is where we are going to view how much our property is worth, as well as how much debt we have on that property. From those two numbers we are also going to be able to see our equity in the property. Also on a balance sheet will be how much cash a property has in its bank account ready to pay for unexpected expenses, or if it has any reserves built up ready to pay for repairs if any are needed.

While a proforma will include elements of both the Profit and Loss and the balance sheet, it will not use the full report for these to financial statements.

The full picture for a proforma should have more to it than the above. A proforma should look like this:

Income Statement:

> Income
> - Expenses
> = NOI
> - Debt
> = Cash flow

Balance Sheet:

> Property Value
> - Debt balance
> = Equity

You see how we have added the equity in the property to what we are looking at when we analyze our proforma? This will give us a more holistic view of how our investment is performing. It will also show us how much money we have made behind the scenes that we have not yet had deposited into our bank accounts. These are profits that require a little work to access. We either have to sell the property or refi the property in order to access these profits and turn them into cash in our bank.

But still, we are only looking at a single time period and we know that we are going to hold an investment property for much more than a year. We could hold the property for the rest of our lives! The standard period to look at a property is for 5 years, so let's see what that looks like.

Year	1	2	3	4	5
Income					
Expenses					
NOI					
Debt					
Cashflow					
Property Value					
Debt balance					
Equity					

This is what a template looks like. Let's run through an example. We buy a property that has $100,000 annual income. It has $40,000 annual expenses.

Warning: we are about to do some math. If you would rather watch this process on a video than read it, go to **Haydencrabtree.com/resources** and if you want to get a simple deal calculator to help out in your future deals, go to HaydenCrabtree.com/Calculator to get it for free.

If you would like to read through, keep going! I would recommend reading through first then watching the video!

Year	1	2	3	4	5
Income	$100,000.00				
Expenses	-$40,000.00				
NOI					
Debt					
Cashflow					
Property Value					
Debt balance					
Equity					

What is the NOI going to be?

Year	1	2	3	4	5
Income	$100,000.00				
Expenses	-$40,000.00				
NOI	$60,000.00				
Debt					
Cashflow					
Property Value					
Debt balance					
Equity					

That's right, $60,000.

Now that we have the NOI, we can know what the value is.

Now let's say we bought this property on a 6% cap. How much did we pay?

Year	1	2	3	4	5
Income	$100,000.00				
Expenses	-$40,000.00				
NOI	$60,000.00				
Debt					
Cashflow					
Property Value	$1,000,000.00				
Debt balance					
Equity					

$1,000,000 is the value.

See how we are combining the cash flow element of the property in addition to valuation of a property? That is what a proforma is all about. Looking at both cash flow and value at the same time.

Really what we want to look at is equity, because as investors the equity we have in a property is more important than the value of the property itself.

Now, let's say we used 80% LTV on this $1,000,000 purchase. What is our debt balance?

Year	1	2	3	4	5
Income	$100,000.00				
Expenses	-$40,000.00				
NOI	$60,000.00				
Debt					
Cashflow					
Property Value	$1,000,000.00				
Debt balance	-$800,000.00				
Equity					

$800,000. We borrowed $800k from the bank and we had to put in the rest. So, how much equity is in the property at the start?

Year	1	2	3	4	5
Income	$100,000.00				
Expenses	-$40,000.00				
NOI	$60,000.00				
Debt					
Cashflow					
Property Value	$1,000,000.00				
Debt balance	-$800,000.00				
Equity	$200,000.00				

$200,000! 20% of the purchase price. Making sense so far?

Now we want to figure out what our cash flow is going to be. So we have to calculate our debt. Let's say we get a 30 year amortizing loan at 5% interest. The payment on this is going to be $52,041 a year. I calculated this using the information in the debt section of this book. If you like excel or google sheets you can also do it using the following formula = PMT(0.05,30,-800000)

Year	1	2	3	4	5
Income	$100,000.00				
Expenses	-$40,000.00				
NOI	$60,000.00				
Debt	-$52,041.15				
Cashflow					
Property Value	$1,000,000.00				
Debt balance	-$800,000.00				
Equity	$200,000.00				

Now we can subtract our debt from our NOI to get our cash flow.

Year	1	2	3	4	5
Income	$100,000.00				
Expenses	-$40,000.00				
NOI	$60,000.00				
Debt	-$52,041.15				
Cashflow	$7,958.85				
Property Value	$1,000,000.00				
Debt balance	-$800,000.00				
Equity	$200,000.00				

So after our expenses and our debt, we are going to cash flow $7,958.85 a year.

Awesome! We have just completed year one of our proforma! We should be able to get the numbers for year one of an investment very easily. Now that we have year one, we need to move on to looking at year two and what we can expect out of the property in year 2. This will require a little more thought.

Let's say this investment is a 10 unit apartment complex that has no room for improvements and the rent on the units are $833 a month. We are buying this property and we are going to ride the inflation wave. Let's see what our proforma looks like for year 2.

First, our income is going to increase by the amount of inflation, 2%. This will take the income from \$100,000 to \$102,000. See proforma

Year	1	2	3	4	5
Income	\$100,000.00	\$102,000.00			
Expenses	-\$40,000.00				
NOI	\$60,000.00				
Debt	-\$52,041.15				
Cashflow	\$7,958.85				
Property Value	\$1,000,000.00				
Debt balance	-\$800,000.00				
Equity	\$200,000.00				

At the same time, our expenses are going to increase by 2% too. All I did is \$40,000 X 1.02

Year	1	2	3	4	5
Income	\$100,000.00	\$102,000.00			
Expenses	-\$40,000.00	-\$40,800.00			
NOI	\$60,000.00				
Debt	-\$52,041.15				
Cashflow	\$7,958.85				
Property Value	\$1,000,000.00				
Debt balance	-\$800,000.00				
Equity	\$200,000.00				

So now that we have our income and expenses, we can get our year 2 NOI.

Year	1	2	3	4	5
Income	\$100,000.00	\$102,000.00			
Expenses	-\$40,000.00	-\$40,800.00			
NOI	\$60,000.00	\$61,200.00			
Debt	-\$52,041.15				
Cashflow	\$7,958.85				
Property Value	\$1,000,000.00				
Debt balance	-\$800,000.00				
Equity	\$200,000.00				

Look at that! Even though income and expenses both increased by 2%, we still had NOI growth. This is a powerful concept to understand. Even though income and expenses grew at the same rate, because income was a larger number than expense, it grew by a bigger dollar amount and the result is that you are going to have a bigger NOI.

Now let's skip down to property value for a second before we plug in our cash flow.

Let's take our new year 2 NOI and see what happened to our property value on the 6% cap rate. So divide $61,200 by 6%

Year	1	2	3	4	5
Income	$100,000.00	$102,000.00			
Expenses	-$40,000.00	-$40,800.00			
NOI	$60,000.00	$61,200.00			
Debt	-$52,041.15				
Cashflow	$7,958.85				
Property Value	$1,000,000.00	$1,020,000.00			
Debt balance	-$800,000.00				
Equity	$200,000.00				

Wow! Just by inflation occurring, our property appreciated by $20,000. Do you see how in a proforma you have a full picture of both the cash flow and the value and how the two are interconnected?

Now, let's jump back up to the debt and cash flow. *Our debt payment is not going to change.* It is going to stay the same at $52,041.15. What will our cash flow be in year 2?

Year	1	2	3	4	5
Income	$100,000.00	$102,000.00			
Expenses	-$40,000.00	-$40,800.00			
NOI	$60,000.00	$61,200.00			
Debt	-$52,041.15	-$52,041.15			
Cashflow	$7,958.85	$9,158.85			
Property Value	$1,000,000.00	$1,020,000.00			
Debt balance	-$800,000.00				
Equity	$200,000.00				

Our projected cash flow for year 2 is $9,158.85. This represents **a 15% increase** from year one, even though we only had a 2% increase in inflation.

Is this the only way we made money? Nope, we also benefited from our debt being paid down. As we now know, the first year is going to be the smallest pay down of any year because of how a loan works. I'll do the math for us based off of that spreadsheet I referred to earlier.

Year	1	2	3	4	5
Income	$100,000.00	$102,000.00			
Expenses	-$40,000.00	-$40,800.00			
NOI	$60,000.00	$61,200.00			
Debt	-$52,041.15	-$52,041.15			
Cashflow	$7,958.85	$9,158.85			
Property Value	$1,000,000.00	$1,020,000.00			
Debt balance	-$800,000.00	-$787,958.85			
Equity	$200,000.00				

So, even though this is our lowest year ever, we still benefited from a $12,041.15 reduction in the balance of our loan. What is our equity in the property at the end of year 2? All we have to do is take the property value and subtract out the debt balance.

Year	1	2	3	4	5
Income	$100,000.00	$102,000.00			
Expenses	-$40,000.00	-$40,800.00			
NOI	$60,000.00	$61,200.00			
Debt	-$52,041.15	-$52,041.15			
Cashflow	$7,958.85	$9,158.85			
Property Value	$1,000,000.00	$1,020,000.00			
Debt balance	-$800,000.00	-$787,958.85			
Equity	$200,000.00	$232,041.15			

Our new equity in the property has increased to $232,041.15. Are you following this?

From year 1 to year 2 we made over $32,000 in equity from appreciation through inflation and debt pay down. In addition we made almost $10,000 in cash flow into our pocket!

This is the basis of a proforma.

Now what we want to do is play this same thing out over 5 years. See below for the full 5 year picture. All we did here was multiply the income and expenses by 1.02 each year and reduce the debt we owe. If you want to do this yourself, I would recommend MyPropertyStats.Com calculator. Or if you want a simple and free version, just visit HaydenCrabtree.com/Calculator to get your hands on it.

Year	1	2	3	4	5
Income	$100,000.00	$102,000.00	$104,040.00	$106,120.80	$108,243.22
Expenses	-$40,000.00	-$40,800.00	-$41,616.00	-$42,448.32	-$43,297.29
NOI	$60,000.00	$61,200.00	$62,424.00	$63,672.48	$64,945.93
Debt	-$52,041.15	-$52,041.15	-$52,041.15	-$52,041.15	-$52,041.15
Cashflow	$7,958.85	$9,158.85	$10,382.85	$11,631.33	$12,904.78
Property Value	$1,000,000.00	$1,020,000.00	$1,040,400.00	$1,061,208.00	$1,082,432.16
Debt balance	-$800,000.00	-$787,958.85	-$775,315.65	-$762,040.28	-$748,101.15
Equity	$200,000.00	$232,041.15	$265,084.35	$299,167.72	$334,331.01

At the start of this investment, our Income was $100,000, our NOI was $60,000, our cash flow was just under $8,000, our property value was $1M and our equity was $200k.

At the end of year 5 all of those numbers have increased, our annual cash flow is close to $13,000, our property value is over $1,080,000, and our equity has gone from $200k to $334k.

If we would have sold this property in year 5, we would have gotten a total of $52k in cash flow, and made another $134k in equity increase.

This is why they say, "Don't wait to buy real estate. Buy real estate and wait."

Looking at this 5 year picture is called underwriting, and this specific analysis is a proforma.

CHAPTER 49

VALUE ADD INVESTING

N ow that we have this knowledge of how to underwrite, we can analyze different options. For example, we can analyze how this investment would look if the current rents on these units are $833, but they should really be at $1,000 for each unit a month.

How would we analyze that investment? Well first we would realize that the only factor we really need to change in this proforma is the income line. We are going to have 10 units at $1,000 each a month, for 12 months. Our new income will be: 10 units X $1,000 X 12 months = $120,000 a year. We also need to realize that this will take us some time to raise the rents, so let's say this income change does not take place in full until year 2.

Year	1	2	3	4	5
Income	$100,000.00				
Expenses	-$40,000.00				
NOI	$60,000.00				
Debt	-$52,041.15				
Cashflow	$7,958.85				
Property Value	$1,000,000.00				
Debt balance	-$800,000.00				
Equity	$200,000.00				

So year 1 is going to be exactly the same. We are going to finance the property the same way, our income, expenses, debt, cash flow, and value are all going to be the same. But now we raise the income to $120,000 in year 2.

Year	1	2	3	4	5
Income	$100,000.00	$120,000.00			
Expenses	-$40,000.00	-$40,800.00			
NOI	$60,000.00				
Debt	-$52,041.15				
Cashflow	$7,958.85				
Property Value	$1,000,000.00				
Debt balance	-$800,000.00				
Equity	$200,000.00				

Income goes up, but expenses will still only rise by the rate of inflation. Now we can look at our new NOI after the rate raise.

Year	1	2	3	4	5
Income	$100,000.00	$120,000.00			
Expenses	-$40,000.00	-$40,800.00			
NOI	$60,000.00	$79,200.00			
Debt	-$52,041.15				
Cashflow	$7,958.85				
Property Value	$1,000,000.00				
Debt balance	-$800,000.00				
Equity	$200,000.00				

Our NOI jumped, so let's look at our new cash flow:

Year	1	2	3	4	5
Income	$100,000.00	$120,000.00			
Expenses	-$40,000.00	-$40,800.00			
NOI	$60,000.00	$79,200.00			
Debt	-$52,041.15	-$52,041.15			
Cashflow	$7,958.85	$27,158.85			
Property Value	$1,000,000.00				
Debt balance	-$800,000.00				
Equity	$200,000.00				

All of the additional monies from the rate raise goes to the NOI, but it will not affect our debt payments, so it gets passed on directly to our cash flow. This is money that we get to keep!

Because our NOI went up, let's also take a look at our new value. We will still be using a 6% cap rate, as our NOI changed, but our cap rate will stay the same

Year	1	2	3	4	5
Income	$100,000.00	$120,000.00			
Expenses	-$40,000.00	-$40,800.00			
NOI	$60,000.00	$79,200.00			
Debt	-$52,041.15	-$52,041.15			
Cashflow	$7,958.85	$27,158.85			
Property Value	$1,000,000.00	$1,320,000.00			
Debt balance	-$800,000.00	-$787,958.85			
Equity	$200,000.00	$532,041.15			

Our new value for the property after the rate raise is $1,320,000! After our debt paydown that is going to translate into over half a million dollars in equity.

This kind of investing is called value add investing. The whole reason we underwrite and use a proforma to analyze these investments is to understand what the property could be once we add value to the property.

Value add investing allows you to operate the property better than the previous owner and therefore increase the value of the property due to a higher NOI.

At year 2, we have already added a lot of value to the property, but we will still get the benefits of inflation and debt paydown going forward. Let's take a look at where we are after 5 years by continuing to multiply income and expenses by 1.02 for inflation.

Year	1	2	3	4	5
Income	$100,000.00	$120,000.00	$122,400.00	$124,848.00	$127,344.96
Expenses	-$40,000.00	-$40,800.00	-$41,616.00	-$42,448.32	-$43,297.29
NOI	$60,000.00	$79,200.00	$80,784.00	$82,399.68	$84,047.67
Debt	-$52,041.15	-$52,041.15	-$52,041.15	-$52,041.15	-$52,041.15
Cashflow	$7,958.85	$27,158.85	$28,742.85	$30,358.53	$32,006.53
Property Value	$1,000,000.00	$1,320,000.00	$1,346,400.00	$1,373,328.00	$1,400,794.56
Debt balance	-$800,000.00	-$787,958.85	-$775,315.65	-$762,040.28	-$748,101.15
Equity	$200,000.00	$532,041.15	$571,084.35	$611,287.72	$652,693.41

In this example, which is very doable in the real world, we have taken $200,000 and turned it into more than $650,000 in equity! That does not include cash flow, or tax benefits!

One thing to note is the equity amount is not a benefit we get every year. It would be the amount we would receive if we were to sell the property in that year. So if we sold in year 2 we could get $532,041. If we sold in year 5 we could get $652,693. We do not get $532,041 in year 2 and $652,693 in year 5. Make sense?

To recap:

1. We put $200,000 down on the property.
2. We raised the rents from $833 a month to $1,000 a month. That made our income go from $100,000 a year to $120,000 a year.
3. The raised income made our NOI go up.
4. The NOI going up made our property value go up. The value of the property went from $1,000,000 in year 1 to $1,400,794 in year 5.
5. Our NOI went up, but our debt payments stayed the same. Our cash flow went from $7,958 in year 1 to $32,006 in year 5.
6. We turned $200,000 into $652,693 of equity in just 5 years!

This may seem challenging to do on your own, but I promise it is all very simple math. In order to help you analyze a property and create your own proforma I have made a template for you that can shortcut you to success at the link below.

Again, to watch all these steps and explanation on a video, go to **Haydencrabtree.com/Resources** and if you want to get the free calculator, go to **HaydenCrabtree.com/Calculator**

UNDERSTANDING RETURNS

L et's stop for a second and do a ROI check in. ROI stands for Return on Investment. Do you feel like the knowledge you have learned in this book is worth the price you paid? My goal here is to make sure you walk away from reading this book saying you would have paid 100X what you actually did and it still would have been a good deal. I hope you have learned so much that your brain is about to explode… in a good way :) Let's keep it going!

Speaking of ROI's, in this chapter we are going to use the knowledge we have learned from the proforma to understand some different return metrics so that you can compare one investment to another, and use this as a guide to decide on where you should spend your time and money.

CHAPTER 50

MAKE A DECISION

Let's think for a minute about what our life would look like if we did not use financial returns to guide our decision making process. Let's compare the opportunity in the last chapter where we took the rents from $833 to $1,000 a month and compare it to the following opportunity. They both cost $1,000,000 and require $200,000 in upfront equity. In this new deal, we are in a market where the rents grow at 6% instead of 2%. We were also able to get a lower interest rate on our bank loan which resulted in our debt payments and pay down being different. Which do you choose?

Option 1—from last chapter

Year	1	2	3	4	5
Income	$100,000.00	$120,000.00	$122,400.00	$124,848.00	$127,344.96
Expenses	-$40,000.00	-$40,800.00	-$41,616.00	-$42,448.32	-$43,297.29
NOI	$60,000.00	$79,200.00	$80,784.00	$82,399.68	$84,047.67
Debt	-$52,041.15	-$52,041.15	-$52,041.15	-$52,041.15	-$52,041.15
Cashflow	$7,958.85	$27,158.85	$28,742.85	$30,358.53	$32,006.53
Property Value	$1,000,000.00	$1,320,000.00	$1,346,400.00	$1,373,328.00	$1,400,794.56
Debt balance	-$800,000.00	-$787,958.85	-$775,315.65	-$762,040.28	-$748,101.15
Equity	$200,000.00	$532,041.15	$571,084.35	$611,287.72	$652,693.41

Option 2—new scenario where rents grow at 6%

Year	1	2	3	4	5
Income	$100,000.00	$106,000.00	$112,360.00	$119,101.60	$126,247.70
Expenses	-$40,000.00	-$40,800.00	-$41,616.00	-$42,448.32	-$43,297.29
NOI	$60,000.00	$65,200.00	$70,744.00	$76,653.28	$82,950.41
Debt	-$44,327.99	-$44,327.99	-$44,327.99	-$44,327.99	-$44,327.99
Cashflow	$15,667.75	$20,867.75	$26,411.75	$32,321.03	$38,618.16
Property Value	$1,000,000.00	$1,086,666.67	$1,179,066.67	$1,277,554.67	$1,382,506.83
Debt balance	-$800,000.00	-$789,672.01	-$778,905.08	-$767,680.56	-$755,978.99
Equity	$200,000.00	$296,994.66	$400,161.59	$509,874.11	$626,527.84

Making a decision can be hard if we do not use metrics to help us.

In scenario one, the property is worth more at the end of the 5 years. The second deal has more cash flow at the beginning, then the first deal has more cash flow in year 2–year 3. Then the second deal takes over again in year 4 with more cash flow.

There is no clear answer on which deal is better if you are looking at just the proforma.

Without having a method to decide which deal you would choose, you may end up making the wrong decision. Both deals seem to be great, but they make their money at different speeds. The first deal makes a majority of its money between year 1 and year 2, while the 2nd deal takes longer to make its money because it has a slower increase in income.

We are about to discuss the how to make a decision between the two. Once you learn the fundamentals, you need a system to start putting these decision into practice. That's why inside of My Property Stats, I created two features that will help you. The first feature is a pipeline of all your deals. In a matter of seconds you can compare one deal against another to choose which is going to be a better place to invest your money.

The next feature I added was the ability to compare scenarios within the same deal. Let's say you are wanting to buy a deal. You could either leave it as is or invest some extra money to increase the rents and value. Which should you choose? My Property Stats will let you easily compare the two options and help you choose which one is going to make you the most money.

CHAPTER 51

TIME AND MONEY

I f we do not back our decision in math, then we could make mistakes, mistakes that could end up costing us millions of dollars over our lives…

This is why, as investors, we have to know and live by our financial returns. There are a few return metrics for you to learn here, but first you need to understand a fundamental to wealth that few people understand. This fundamental is called the time value of money (TVM).

What TVM tells us is that a dollar today is worth more than a dollar tomorrow. That is because if we have a dollar today, we can invest it and have it grow each and every day.

So if you have $100 and you can invest it at 10% a year, then in a year you will have $110. If you do that again for another year, you will have $121, not $120. You are going to earn a return on the money that you got back from the initial investment, making your investment grow faster and faster.

This is called compound interest. Here is what $100 at 10% a year looks like on non compound interest vs compound interest.

10%	Non compounding	Compounding
Year 0	$100.00	$100.00
Year 1	$110.00	$110.00
Year 2	$120.00	$121.00
Year 3	$130.00	$133.10
Year 4	$140.00	$146.41
Year 5	$150.00	$161.05
Year 6	$160.00	$177.16
Year 7	$170.00	$194.87
Year 8	$180.00	$214.36
Year 9	$190.00	$235.79
Year 10	$200.00	$259.37

In this chart, notice how the non compounding amount goes up every year by the same amount, $10. But on the right, the money is increasing at a faster pace each year.

When you do not reinvest your earnings, you will still have an investment amount of $100. When you do reinvest your earnings, the amount you are earning interest on will go up each year. This will make my investment grow by a larger amount each year.

When we are talking about $100, it doesn't sound like much. The difference at the end of 10 years is $200 vs $259, so what? Well what if we are investing $100,000 or $1,000,000? In the case of investing a million, now we are talking about a difference of over half a million dollars.

You see, when most people think about a return, they think: "how much did I invest, and how much did I receive?"

If you made an investment for $10,000 and you received back $15,000, what was your return on that investment? Most people will tell you you made a 50% return and this makes sense, right?

$$\frac{\$15,000}{\$10,000} = 150\% \text{ or } 50\% \text{ return}$$

The maths seems to look good to me.

Now what if you invested $10,000 and did not get that $15,000 back until 5 years later, did you still earn a 50% return? The common answer would be yes, but in reality your return per year was much lower every year.

"Oh, I get it!" You're thinking. "I made $5,000 over 5 years. So really I made $1,000 a year."

$5,000 for 5 years. That's $1,000 a year.

$$\frac{\$1,000}{\$10,000} = 10\% \text{ return}$$

"My return on investment in this case is really 10%, not 50%"

While we are getting closer, but we are still wrong. You did not make 10% a year because your money is supposed to grow at a compounding rate like the chart showed us.

In reality you made less than 10% a year. To make 10% a year, you would have had to receive $16,105 as a payment in year 5.

See here. For a 10% a year return, I need to multiply each amount by 10%.

Year 0 = $10,000
Year 1 = $11,000
Year 2 = $12,100
Year 3 = $13,310
Year 4 = $14,641
Year 5 = $16,105

To do this math for yourself, simply multiply 1.1 by the year prior.

If you paid the $10,000 and got back $15,000 in 5 years, TVM tells us the reality is that you are only getting an 8.45% compounding return on your money.

All of a sudden your investment that was a 50% return is now less than 10% a year.

My reason for telling you this is because you need to be educated on what is really happening with your money. You also need to understand that different investment opportunities are going to provide financial benefits in different ways. Like our comparison of the two examples above, one may have more cash flow sooner, with the other providing more equity.

One may return $100 in 2 years, and the other returns double that amount but it takes 6 years. One could have greater tax benefits, while the other has less tax benefits.

The list goes on and on. You need a way to make decisions that are backed in logic, not just gut feelings.

With all these numbers flying around, how do you know how to make a decision that will make you the most money?

CHAPTER 52

INTERNAL RATE OF RETURN

For my finance nerds out there who know about IRR, you can skip this chapter. If "IRR" looks like a foreign language to you, please continue reading this chapter.

You need to start using the Internal Rate of Return (IRR) metric to measure your wealth and how fast your money is growing. IRR measures how much your money grows each year from where it was the year before. It looks at your money and says it should be compounded each year, and will give you the % number for which each deal grows.

What is so great about the IRR is that it can look at very complex equations and give you a simple number to use as a judge. The IRR equation can account for different amounts of money coming in at different times.

In the chapter prior to this one, I said how if you were to invest $10,000 and 5 years later you received $15,000 back that would be a 8.45% return. That 8.45% is the IRR.

I wish I could give you a simple formula for the IRR, but due to its complexity, I cannot. The best way to calculate the IRR is either with a financial calculator, or with an excel or google spreadsheet.

While I wish that I could go more into depth, I fear that I will lose your attention and not be able to clearly communicate exactly how IRR works. For that reason, this chapter is going to be taking place online at the link below.

I have a full video on this at Haydencrabtree.com/resources that will walk through and show the differences in the IRR between the two examples above, and which one you should choose if you were investing your own money for maximum wealth growth.

My hope is that this exercise opens your eyes to the ways in which the 1% look at money that normal people do not. When you realize that your money should compound, you begin to look at your investments differently.

Please go watch the video at Haydencrabtree.com/resources because I am going to show you how to use this for yourself and I feel that you would be cheating your financial education if you did not go watch it.

While in my opinion the IRR trumps all other metrics, we are still going to explain a few other popular metrics that you can use and are simple to calculate.

CHAPTER 53

CASH ON CASH

For the average real estate investor, cash on cash is the most popular metric.

If the property cost $500, with 80% LTV we put in $100, and the bank gave us $400. How much does the property pay us after we pay for our expenses and debt?

If the property paid us $12 a year in cash flow then we would have a 12% cash on cash.

If the property paid us $5 then we would have a 5% cash on cash.

The cash on cash metrics measure how much in annual cash flow you receive for every dollar in equity you had to spend up front.

$$\text{Cash on Cash} = \frac{\text{Annual cash flow}}{\text{Equity required to buy property}}$$

The cash on cash measurement does not care how much you bought the property for. It only cares about how much money you personally had to put in.

Because of the way we can buy properties using a bank's money, we may not get the full picture of how much annual cash flow we are going to get by looking at the NOI and cap rate. We have to analyze the numbers and look at how much we receive every year in cash and how much we had to put into the property.

This is only measuring and comparing cash flow, no other benefits of the real estate investment are considered in the cash on cash measurement.

We do expect the annual cash on cash number to change as our investment performs differently every year.

Here is a proforma that shows how the cash on cash changes each year.

Year	1	2	3	4	5
Income	$100,000.00	$106,000.00	$112,360.00	$119,101.60	$126,247.70
Expenses	-$40,000.00	-$40,800.00	-$41,616.00	-$42,448.32	-$43,297.29
NOI	$60,000.00	$65,200.00	$70,744.00	$76,653.28	$82,950.41
Debt	-$44,327.99	-$44,327.99	-$44,327.99	-$44,327.99	-$44,327.99
Cashflow	$15,667.75	$20,867.75	$26,411.75	$32,321.03	$38,618.16
Property Value	$1,000,000.00	$1,086,666.67	$1,179,066.67	$1,277,554.67	$1,382,506.83
Debt balance	-$800,000.00	-$789,672.01	-$778,905.08	-$767,680.56	-$755,978.99
Equity	$200,000.00	$296,994.66	$400,161.59	$509,874.11	$626,527.84
Cash on cash	7.83%	10.43%	13.21%	16.16%	19.31%

As you can see from this example, our cash on cash changes each year and more than doubles from year 1 to year 5 from 7.83% to 19.31%.

In year 1 we had $15,667.75 of cash flow and the equity required was $200,000. So we take $15,667.75 divided by $200,000 to get 7.83%.

In year 5 we had $38,618.16 of cash flow. The equity required is still $200,000. So we take $38,618.16 divided by $200,000 to get 19.31%.

The cash on cash metric is a good one to use if you are trying to compare financing alternatives and what is going to be best for your cash flow.

For example, if one bank wanted to lend to you at 70% LTV, 5% interest, on a 20 year amortization and the other bank wanted to lend to you at a

80% LTV 5.5% interest on a 25 year amortization, you could use the cash on cash metric to compare which loan option you should take to maximize your cash flow.

	Option 1
	70% LTV
	5% interest
	20 year AM
My Equity	$300,000.00
Bank	$700,000.00
Annual payments	$56,169.81
NOI	$75,000.00
Annual cashflow	$18,830.19
Cash on Cash	**6.28%**

As you can see in option 1, we put $300,000 into the property. This is found beside "My Equity." We then borrowed the other $700,000 from the bank. Because we borrowed $700,000, we have annual payments of $56,169.81.

The NOI on the property is $75,000, so to get our cash flow we are going to subtract the debt payments from the NOI.

$75,000 - $56,169.81 = $18,830.19 is our cash flow.

Now we want to take our cash flow and see how much that is as a percentage of the $300,000 we put in.

$$\frac{\$18,830.19}{\$300,000} = 6.28\%$$

Our cash on cash in this scenario is 6.28%.

Now let's compare that to the next option.

	Option 1	Option 2
	70% LTV	80 % LTV
	5% interest	5.5% interest
	20 year AM	25 Year AM
My Equity	$300,000.00	$200,000.00
Bank	$700,000.00	$800,000.00
Annual payments	$56,169.81	$59,639.48
NOI	$75,000.00	$75,000.00
Annual cashflow	$18,830.19	$15,360.52
Cash on Cash	**6.28%**	**7.68%**

In option 2, we have a longer amortization period, a higher interest rate, and also a higher LTV. Because we have a higher LTV, it means the money we have to put into the property is less. Now instead of putting in $300,000, we only had to put in $200,000.

Because we borrowed more money, our debt payments are higher. The property has the same NOI, so to calculate our cash on cash we are going to do the same thing as we did before.

$75,000 - $59,639.48 = $15,360.52 cash flow

To get out cash on cash, we take $15,360.52 and divide it by how much we put into the property.

$$\frac{\$15,360.52}{\$200,000} = 7.68\%$$

In the first option, we had $18,830.19 of cash flow and in the second option we had $15,360.52. But because we put less money into the deal on option #2, we have a higher cash on cash.

Even though we made less cash flow in option #2, we had a higher cash on cash because we had to put in less money.

You are making more cash flow each year with option 1, but you are making a lower cash on cash because you had to put down more money. With option 2 you are making less cash flow, but that money cost you less in terms of how much you had to put down up front.

So what the cash on cash tells us is how to optimize our cash flow for the money that we do have. If your goal is to build a lot of cash flow then you should be aiming to choose the deals and financing options that give you the highest cash on cash.

CHAPTER 54

ADDING TAX BENEFITS TO YOUR RETURNS

It is not very common for a real estate investor to add tax benefits into a proforma or return metrics for a property. I have never understood why this is not common practice. The main reason that I can think of is that tax benefits are going to vary from investor to investor, like a debt payment will.

The benefits that a high income earner is going to receive from $100,000 of depreciation is going to yield a different result than it is going to for someone only making $50,000 a year. Mainly because of tax brackets and different tax credits.

It is worthwhile for an investor when underwriting a property to consult their accountant and talk about what kind of tax benefits they can expect for a certain type of property. From there they could add those tax benefits into the proforma and truly compare apples to apples.

You could for example have a piece of land that is leased and you could earn 12% cash on cash for that investment. But let's say for the same equity investment you could have bought an apartment complex. At first glance that apartment complex may yield 10% cash on cash, but what if after depreciation it allowed the investor to recoup 50% of their money in the first year through shielding their taxes.

While the land has a higher cash on cash and looks like a better investment at first, you may find out that because of the tax benefits the apartments offer (that the land does not), you come off better at the end of the day.

For that reason I advocate having an additional line at the bottom of your proforma where you add back how much you will save in taxes

Do not underestimate how juicy tax benefits can be for your deals!

CHAPTER 55

HOW LEVERAGE AFFECTS YOUR RETURNS

In this section we have focused on the return of your money rather than the return of the entire real estate project. If we would have used no debt to assist us in buying these projects, then the project returns would be equal to the return on our money.

If we have a good project with a nice return, and we have the full $1,000,000 to spend on the project some people would think to themselves that they should skip using the bank's money because they will get a higher return on the project without using debt.

This mindset will slow down your wealth growth tremendously.

Not only would that allow you to do less projects, it would also cause you to have lower returns overall. When we can use a bank's money to do more projects, and also earn a higher return, we call this Positive Leverage.

No debt
Project $1M
Our Cash $1M

With Debt
Project $1M
Bank $800K
Our cash $200K

20%

100%

Project return 12%
Our return 12%

Project Return 12%
Bank Return 6%
Our return 18%

However, we do have to be aware that leverage can work in the opposite way too.

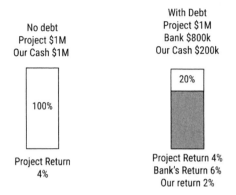

In the above example, our debt costs us more than our project earns us. This actually decreases our returns on the property. When debt hurts us like this, it is called negative leverage and is not good. Stay away from negative leverage.

To find out what the bank is going to get, we need to look at the cost of both the interest and the principal we are paying them on an annual basis. This is called the mortgage constant and is simply:

$$\text{Mortgage constant} = \frac{12 \times \text{Monthly Payment}}{\text{Loan amount}}$$

If we borrowed $100,000 and our monthly payment was $952, what would our mortgage constant be?

$$\text{Mortgage constant} = \frac{12 \times \$952}{\$100,000}$$

$$\text{Mortgage constant} = \frac{\$11,424}{\$100,000}$$

$$\text{Mortgage constant} = 11.42\%$$

Once you get your mortgage constant you can make yourself aware of whether getting debt is beneficial to you on this project or not. If you know that your mortgage constant is 11.42%, then you are looking for projects that return more than that.

Another way to quickly find out if your project makes sense and meets these criteria is to see if your cap rate is higher than the mortgage constant. Your cap rate is going to be equal to your cash on cash if you use no debt. As long as the mortgage constant is less than the cap rate, you will have positive leverage.

Fair warning that the mortgage constant has to be applied with some thought. If you have a value add project with a 2% cash on cash in year 1 and then a 15% cash on cash in year 2, you could have negative leverage year 1 and positive leverage in year 2.

This is where you have to be aware of how your project is going to work out. But if the project is never going to have positive leverage then I would suggest you walk away from that property and find somewhere else to spend your time, energy and money.

CHAPTER 56

CONCLUSION ON RETURNS

The most important takeaway from this section for you to realize is that you need to guide your investments backed in logic and math. While it is important that you have a good feeling about a deal, you also need to make sure the numbers work. If you have bad cash on cash or IRR, you need to spend your money and time on another project that will grow your wealth faster.

Each return measurement has its advantages and disadvantages. Read this chapter again several times until you fully understand how returns work. Once you understand how returns work and what each of them means, your competence and confidence as a real estate investor will rise dramatically. Because you know what you are looking at and how to make the right decision with your time and money, your decision making ability will go up.

The next best step for you is to get your hands on a real estate calculator (or deal analyzer – whatever you want to call it). The one I am using everyday is My Property Stats. Not just because I made it, but because it truly is the best solution I know of. The more you can learn about analyzing properties and financial returns, the higher your financial IQ will be. The higher your financial IQ, the more money you will make.

The My Property Stats deal calculator tells you the IRR, cash on cash and how much you should pay for a property based off of what kind of return you want. Having so much of the process automated for you will save you hundreds of hours, headaches, will give you confidence in your numbers and allow you to win more deals.

This program is so powerful because it will allow you to see what happens to your returns under several scenarios, such as what happens if my rents increase by 3% instead of 2%, or what happens if I upgrade some of my rental units and can therefore charge higher rents. To get this for yourself and start dominating deal analysis, go to MyPropertyStats.Com and hit "register now"

PUTTING IT ALL TOGETHER

You have learned a tremendous amount so far. For sticking through this I want to give you a reward. The reward you are about to get is my exact business model I am using today and intend to use forever. This is the overarching strategy that I use to guide my personal real estate investments.

I call this the "Free Real Estate Playbook." Sounds pretty awesome, right!? Well, it is.

In this section you are going to learn a method you can use to get real estate for free! This method is going to help you scale your real estate business faster than you ever could have imagined. Let me show you how!

Without having learned all the basics that you have learned up until this point, you would not be able to understand how this is possible. You would think this section is a trick. That being said, if you skipped any of the prior chapters, please go back and read those so you can take full advantage of what we are about to show here. If you do not understand the fundamentals you cannot understand how they work together to make this possible.

Get your notebook ready, this is life changing!

Let's do this!!

CHAPTER 57

FREE REAL ESTATE

First, let's define our goal: You want to own cash flow real estate that will pay you each month for the rest of your life, and you want to do it with none of your own money. Sure, we could do it with our own money, but we will eventually run out of our own money, no matter how much we have. If we could use the bank's money to do it instead of our own, that would be much better. The banks are not going to run out of money anytime soon.

Let's begin with our property. We are going to seek out a value add property.

Because we are all familiar with this, we will go with an apartment complex.

We seek out an apartment complex that is currently underperforming. It could be underperforming for many reasons, but we recognize that this property could have a much higher NOI than it currently does.

The example we will use: property has a current NOI of $64,000 a year, and because it needs some love, we can buy it on an 8% cap rate for $800,000. This is represented by the following image.

Property
$800K
$64,000 NOI

8%
Cap rate

As we know, we can go to the bank and ask them for an 80% LTV loan. They see the potential in this property, so they agree to give you the loan. They lend you 80% of $800,000 = $640,000.

Now you have a great property ready to buy and ready to add some value. You have a bank ready to loan you 80% of the project at 5% interest on a 30 year amortization.

You also remembered to negotiate a long balloon period so you do not have to pay your debt off anytime soon.

All you have to do is come up with $160,000 to put in your 20%.

Property
$800k
$64,000 NOI

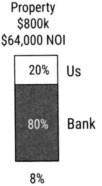

8%
Cap rate

As represented in the image, the bank is going to give you 80% of the purchase in debt and you have to put in 20% equity.

If you have $160,000 that is awesome. You can use your own money and I am going to show you how to get that money back so you have none of your own money in the deal.

If you do not have $160,000, then you can find some investors. I am going to teach you how you can talk to investors. Keep reading and you will learn as we go through this chapter.

So, we are going to buy this property whether it be with our investor's money or with our own. Once we purchase the property we are going to begin working on it and increasing the NOI.

When we are looking to buy the property, we make a proforma. The proforma looks like this:

Year	1	2	3	4	5
Income	$100,000.00				
Expenses	-$36,000.00				
NOI	$64,000.00				
Debt	-$41,632.92				
Cashflow	$22,367.08				
Property Value	$800,000.00				
Debt balance	-$640,000.00				
Equity	$160,000.00				

You knew that the $100,000 of income was extremely low for this property. It has 20 units and they are each renting for $500 a month. But because the property was not being managed well, there were several tenants not paying their rent and living there for free.

While we are looking at the property, we want to find out how much it could make if all units were rented and all customers paid when they were supposed to. This is called "Potential Gross Income."

Potential gross income = monthly rent x number of units

To find the potential gross income for this property we would take the 20 units and multiply that by $500 to get our potential gross income every month.

Potential gross income = $500 x 20 = $10,000 every month

$10,000 x 12 months = $120,000 a year

You knew when you first bought this property that if you could get those bad tenants out, or get them to start paying you could add to the NOI. The property has the potential to make $120,000 a year, but because it was being mismanaged, it was only making $100,000.

You realize this and notice the current owner is missing out on $20,000 a year.

You also realize that the buildings look run down, so if you just cleaned up the trash outside, did some nice landscaping and painted the buildings, you would make the apartments feel nicer, be able to charge more money and attract a higher quality tenant to your building.

You look at your competition and find out that new rents after the buildings are fixed up are going to be $750 a unit.

$750 x 20 = $15,000 a month

$15,000 x 12 months = $180,000 a year

Your new potential gross income after fixing the place up is going to be $180,000 a year.

To do this, you told yourself that you are going to need to spend some money to fix the place up. You learn that you need $30,000 for paint,

$15,000 for landscaping, and $5,000 to pay someone to haul off all the trash laying around.

In addition to buying the property for $800,000, you are going to spend $50,000 fixing the place up. You know that this is an investment in the property, because if we spend the money, it is going to boost our NOI. We tell the bank all of this, and ask them to pay for 80% of our improvements too. So now our proforma looks like this:

Year	1	2	3	4	5
Income	$100,000.00				
Expenses	-$36,000.00				
NOI	$64,000.00				
Debt	-$44,234.98				
Cashflow	$19,765.02				
Property Value	$850,000.00				
Debt balance	-$680,000.00				
Equity	$170,000.00				

Notice how property value went up, debt and equity went up, debt payments went up, and cash flow went down. The cash flow went down because our debt payments went up in year one, but we have not started to receive any additional income until year 2.

Because the bank is going to lend us an extra $40,000, our payments are going to go up. We are also going to have to come up with an extra $10,000 of cash to make the improvements. But this is money that is well spent. We know that our NOI is going to rise significantly in year 2.

To estimate what our NOI, equity value and cash flow in is going to be in year 2, we need to do some math and put the numbers into our proforma that we calculated.

Let's plug that in from the math we did finding out what our new income will be in year 2.

Year	1	2	3	4	5
Income	$100,000.00	$180,000.00			
Expenses	-$36,000.00	-$36,720.00			
NOI	$64,000.00	$143,280.00			
Debt	-$44,234.98	-$44,234.98			
Cashflow	$19,765.02	$99,045.02			
Property Value	$850,000.00				
Debt balance	-$680,000.00				
Equity	$170,000.00				

Our income rose, our expenses went up by the rate of inflation, our debt payment stayed the same, and as a result our NOI and our cash flow went through the roof!

In year 2, we boost our cash on cash return to 58%! What about our equity in the property? What happens to it?

Well as you know, we bought this property at an 8% cap rate. Because it was run down, some tenants weren't paying and the property looked rough, so we got a good deal.

We came in and fixed it up, and also replaced low quality (high risk) tenants with high quality (low risk) tenants.

As a result, we make our property more attractive and a lower risk investment. As a reward for making this property nicer and lower risk, we now get to use a lower cap rate for the property.

So while we bought it as a C class building, we have turned it into a B class building. As we look at what cap we should use, we find that other apartment units similar in size and quality to this investment are being sold at 7% cap rates.

So we value our property now on a 7% cap rate, because that is what the market tells us we should do.

Let's look at the property value on a 7% cap rate using the year 2 NOI:

Year	1	2	3	4	5
Income	$100,000.00	$180,000.00			
Expenses	-$36,000.00	-$36,720.00			
NOI	$64,000.00	$143,280.00			
Debt	-$44,234.98	-$44,234.98			
Cashflow	$19,765.02	$99,045.02			
Property Value	$850,000.00	$2,046,857.14			
Debt balance	-$680,000.00				
Equity	$170,000.00				

WOW! Our new value is over $2,000,000. If we had used an 8% cap rate, the property would have only been worth $1,791,000, but because we made the property lower risk, we changed our cap rate, and boosted the value!

Year	1	2	3	4	5
Income	$100,000.00	$180,000.00			
Expenses	-$36,000.00	-$36,720.00			
NOI	$64,000.00	$143,280.00			
Debt	-$44,234.98	-$44,234.98			
Cashflow	$19,765.02	$99,045.02			
Property Value	$850,000.00	$2,046,857.14			
Debt balance	-$680,000.00	-$669,765.02			
Equity	$170,000.00	$1,377,092.12			

Now at the end of year 2, we have $1,377,092 of equity in the property.

"That's great and all, Hayden, but I already get this. This is *value add investing*. How do I twist this so that I get free real estate?"

Well, in the following illustration we are going to compare the property from year 1 to year 2. The bar on the left represents the property at first. It was worth $850,000 after the renovations. It was 80% leveraged. The clear part of the bar represents equity.

On the right, we have a much larger bar, because the property value has gone up. The debt level (the shaded part) has gone down slightly due to paying down the loan balance. Now, we have a large amount of equity.

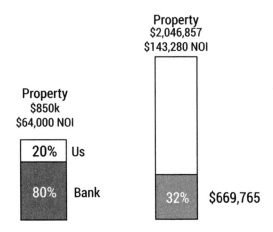

Once you execute on the value add, you have several options, and all of them are good for you.

Look at the image above. The bar on the left represents the property when you first bought it. The equity amount is only 20% so you do not have a lot of options.

If you look at the bar on the right, it represents the property once you have added the value. You have a large amount of equity! This is where you are going to make some amazing money and get free real estate.

Now that the value has been added, the property is worth much more, and your debt has been paid down. Your property sits at 32% LTV. As you know, we can get up to 80% LTV on these investment properties.

The free real estate playbook goes like this: buy a property, add value to the property, go back to the bank to do a cash out refi. I like to do a cash out refi and get just enough money to pay off my first loan, and to pay off my investors their original amount.

It looks like this:

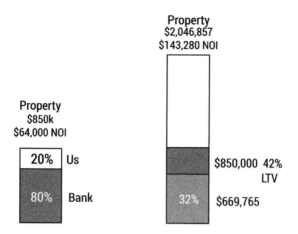

So you go back to the bank at the end of year two and tell my banker, "Hey, banker, thanks so much for lending to me on this apartment building. I have 2 pieces of really good news. The first piece of good news is that the property is doing great and is now worth over $2,000,000. The second piece of good news is that I would like to refinance $850,000."

You see, when you do a refinance at the same level of the original total project cost, you will have enough money coming back to you to pay off the first mortgage and also give my investors all their money back.

Now that we did the refi, we are going to see a jump in the cost of the debt because our loan is now bigger. It will look like this:

Year	1	2	3	4	5
Income	$100,000.00	$180,000.00	$183,600.00		
Expenses	-$36,000.00	-$36,720.00	-$37,454.40		
NOI	$64,000.00	$143,280.00	$146,145.60		
Debt	-$44,234.98	-$44,234.98	-$55,293.72		
Cashflow	$19,765.02	$99,045.02	$90,851.88		
Property Value	$850,000.00	$2,046,857.14	$2,087,794.29		
Debt balance	-$680,000.00	-$669,765.02	-$850,000.00		
Equity	$170,000.00	$1,377,092.12	$1,237,794.29		

Your debt has gone up to $850,000 and because of that, your annual payments are going to rise from $44,234 to $55,293. You can see this change in the debt between year 2 and year 3.

So if you have your own money to do this deal, if you had the $170,000 up front, awesome.

The refinance is going to be $850,000. Out of that money you are going to have to pay off your first loan. Then you can take the rest of that money and put it back into your bank account. Or buy a Ferrari. Or you could bury it in your backyard. Do whatever you want...

Congratulations because *you now have a free piece of real estate.*

You own the property all by yourself at 100%, and you have all of the money you originally used back in your possession to use on whatever you want. And by the way, you have all that money back *tax free*!

You now own a real estate investment that you have no money in, and you are going to make $90,851 in cash flow every single year for the rest of your life. Also, what happens when that debt gets paid off?

That's right, no more debt payments! When you wait the full time period and have your tenants pay your debt off, you get a raise! No more debt payments, as your cash flow will now be equal to your NOI.

So if your NOI was $146,145 after your debt was paid off, you would be able to pocket and keep $146,145 as your cash flow for that year!

If you did not have the $170,000 up front and you partnered with investors, then now is the time that you give your investors all of their money back.

The strategy for bringing investors in looks like this, "Hey Mr. Investor, I know you have a lot of money sitting in your account (losing value daily from inflation) and you need to invest it in good projects. I have a great project I am working on right now but need some equity to make it happen. If you fund the project, I will get you all of your money back in 3-5 years, and after that you will still own a piece of cash flow real estate for the rest of your life that I do all the work on."

You are telling your potential investors that they are going to get their money back in full and they are still going to make cash flow from that for the rest of their life.

Once you get your investor their money back, you can decide what makes sense for the agreement you have. You could tell your investor they are going to get 10% on their original money and make $17,000 year. For your investors they are getting a 10% cash on cash but now have all their money back. This is a great income stream for any investor!

You could tell your investor you will split the cash flow 50/50. From here there are many options and this is where you can cut a deal that makes sense for both you and your investors.

Many investors will wonder why they should invest with you instead of doing it themselves.

While some investors will have time to do it themselves, the truth is many will not, and time should not be a limiting factor for someone to get into real estate as an investment.

As someone who works with investors, you need to clearly understand the value that you bring to the table. In every business venture and partnership, each party will bring some sort of value to the table. Most people think value means only money, but that is not true.

Your time to execute a project is a great form of value that you can bring to a partnership. Expertise in many cases is much more valuable than both time and money.

Don't forget you also can give your investor tax benefits to decrease their tax bill! Wealthy people flush a lot of their money down the drain each year by paying taxes and real estate can help them pay less in taxes. Give your investors a copy of this book so they can read for themselves!

If you can show an investor how they can invest $100,000 in real estate and save $80,000 in taxes in the first year, I think they will be willing to listen to your opportunity.

CHAPTER 58

FULL REFINANCE

A nother option you have after you have added the value to a property would be to take a full refi instead of just refinancing to the level of investor pay off.

We have the same image from before but now we have added a third option. This option is going to visually show us what would happen if we did a full refi instead of a partial refi.

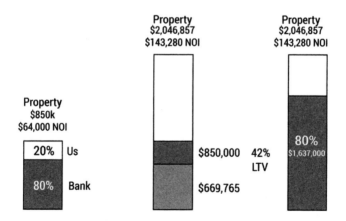

With the property valued at $2,046,857 you could do an 80% refi on this property and receive $1,637,000. You will have to use some of these proceeds to pay off the original loan:

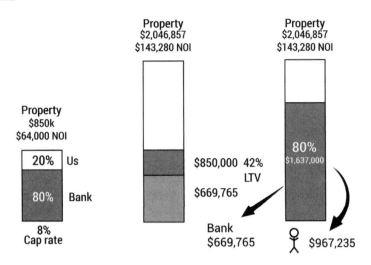

So, out of the $1,637,000, you have to give the orginal bank $669,765.

But even after you pay off your loan, you will have $967,235 in tax free cash!

You could give your investor back double their original money at a $340,000 payoff and keep $627,235 for yourself, <u>AND STILL OWN THE PROPERTY.</u>

After you deposited the $627,235 in your bank account, you would still look to receive cash flow from the property each year. Let's take a look at what that would look like:

Year	1	2	3	4	5
Income	$100,000.00	$180,000.00	$183,600.00		
Expenses	-$36,000.00	-$36,720.00	-$37,454.40		
NOI	$64,000.00	$143,280.00	$146,145.60		
Debt	-$44,234.98	-$44,234.98	-$106,520.80		
Cashflow	$19,765.02	$99,045.02	$39,624.80		
Property Value	$850,000.00	$2,046,857.14	$2,087,794.29		
Debt balance	-$680,000.00	-$669,765.02	-$1,637,485.71		
Equity	$170,000.00	$1,377,092.12	$450,308.57		

Your debt payments would more than double, but you would still get almost $40,000 of cash flow each year, and could expect that to go up over time. In addition to your cash flow, if you were to sell your property, you still have the 20% in equity that would come back to you! That 20% is $450k!

To recap, you or you and your investor:

- Invested $170,000
- Could: A. Get paid off in 2 years and cash flow $94k a year

  B. Do a full refi and take $967k to split between the two of you and still cash flow almost $40k a year
- Sell the property and walk away with another $450k
- Have your tenants pay off your debts for you over the next decades
- Benefit from appreciation and rent growth
- Pay little to no taxes from the deprecation
- Take the $450k of equity and do this whole formula over again tax free with a 1031

Is there anything you can think of that is better than this?

These numbers I am giving you are just an example. You have many options on how to give money back to your investors and earn them a great return once you successfully add value to a property. All of this is made possible by understanding the fundamentals of real estate. If you did not know how cap rates work or how to finance properties this would not be possible for you to understand. Once you understand all of this, the only thing left to do is execute!

HOW YOU CAN START TODAY

So, right now you are probably thinking to yourself that this is great. You are so happy that you read this book, and you are ready to get started capitalizing on the benefits of real estate. Right now you are in one of three situations:

1. You have money but no time
2. You have time but no money
3. You have money and time

I am going to talk about what to do in order to start making progress in the coming chapters depending on which of the three situations you are in.

But before I do that, I wanted to make sure you know I have a second book out now. It called *Skip The Flip: Three Keys To Any Deal*. That book covers

- What the *Three Keys* to any deal are, and how to build your portfolio no matter how much or little money you have
- Different investment strategies and which is right for you
- Where to look to find deals that have great returns and little competition
- The full process to go from "contract to close"
- How to conduct Due Diligence so you never buy a bad investment property
- How to manage deals after you buy them
- How to get deals financed, no matter how much or little money you have.
- The 4 different ways to buy real estate even if you don't have a huge bank account.

If you want the audiobook of that, you can get it at HaydenCrabtree.com/ Audio or for the paperback you can go to Amazon and search "Hayden Crabtree". The cover is black with red accents. If you have enjoyed this book, you will like *Three Keys* even more

No matter which one of these applies to you, you need to understand the three things that are needed to grow your real estate portfolio.

CHAPTER 59

YOU HAVE MONEY BUT NO TIME

This is a lot of the people I talk to. This could be you if you are a lawyer, a doctor, or an engineer. Anyone who enjoys their primary job where they do well financially, but they are getting eaten alive in taxes, and also work a normal work week and do not want to give away all their free time to dealing with real estate. These people want to start building cash flow and pay less in taxes. These are primarily the people who invest in deals with people like me.

In the world of real estate, there are people like me who take investor's money to buy real estate and benefit both parties. I am called the "Sponsor" or "Syndicator."

The investor brings money to the deal, and the sponsor goes out and finds the deal, underwrites the deal, finds the bank to give a loan, buys the property, performs the value add, manages the property and does the refi. The sponsor will also be in charge of overseeing the property's staff, tenant relations and much more.

There is a significant amount of work and knowledge that is needed to be a good syndicator.

This works out well because the investor has a lot of money, but they don't have a lot of time. The investor may have expertise as well, or they may not.

The investors are relying on the sponsor to be reputable and know what they are doing to execute the project.

So if you are a doctor, lawyer, engineer, business executive, entrepreneur, or in any other field that you really enjoy working in and you make good money, but you don't have the time to go out and find, buy, and operate these investments, you may want to team up with a sponsor like myself. While you may have never heard of this before, people like me are out there all over the country buying real estate deals and making them and their investors very wealthy.

One thing to be aware of if you are going to invest with a sponsor: make sure the person has a track record of success. If they have gone to one seminar and watched a couple of youtube videos but never owned a property, you may want to catch up with them on a later deal.

The truth is that there is a lot to be learned in the world of owning and operating real estate, and you do not want to be a sponsor's guinea pig. Questions you should always ask before investing with a sponsor:

- Tell me about your last deal
- What is your strategy
- What markets do you invest in and why
- What legal structure will you be using
- Do I have to be accredited to invest with you
- Tell me about a deal that went bad. How did you handle the failure
- What is the exit strategy

How they should answer

- Tell me about your last deal
  - Talk about whatever they are working on. If they can't answer then they are new and you will be their guinea pig
- What is your strategy

- If they can't quickly tell you how they plan to make money, buckle up because you are in for a scary ride
- What markets do you invest in and why
  - An investor should always know the market (the city in which the property is located) demographics of the deal. Why are they investing in that specific market out of the thousands of cities in America? If they have not paid any attention to the market and are only looking at the deal, proceed with caution. The market is the most important factor to being able to execute a business plan
- What legal structure will you be using
  - If they are not certain, you should be cautious. There is a difference between them not being certain and relying on their legal counsel and them not being certain and having no clear path to certainty. Lawyers are good for both parties. Always be sure to have an operating agreement signed up front that clearly lays out who holds what responsibilities and how everyone will get paid. The legal structure you choose to use will determine how much taxes you pay and what your legal liability is. Always have your legal documents done up front. They are an investment and worth every penny.
- Do I have to be accredited to invest with you
  - To be accredited means to have a net worth of over $1 million excluding your personal residence. You are also accredited if you make $200,000 a year if you are single, or $300,000 a year if you are married. There are many SEC regulations that prohibit a sponsor from taking an investor's money unless they are accredited. There are some loopholes here so ask your sponsor how they plan to handle this. If you are not accredited, you can still invest with a syndicator. You will have to find a syndicator who accepts non accredited investors.
- Tell me about a deal that went bad. How did you handle the failure
  - Life is easy and everyone is high fiving when things go well, but how does the person handling your money behave when things don't go as planned? Do they give up and leave you in the dust?

This is more of a character question that you will be sure you want to ask. Listen to the response closely and imagine what your life would be like with this person if things do not go as planned.

- What is the exit strategy
  - If the sponsor does not have an exit strategy then I would avoid them. Before you enter an investment, you should always ask yourself how and when is this investment going to end? An exit strategy could be a refi, it could be a sale. Saying that you don't have an exit strategy is not an exit strategy.

If you get a fishy feeling from the answer to any of these questions, please proceed with caution.

As an investor, you should be getting yourself into a passive investment that requires little to no time on an ongoing basis while you are still getting the benefits of appreciation, leverage, cash flow, equity build up and tax benefits.

If you have ever heard the term "mailbox money" that is what I am talking about here. When you partner up and invest with a high quality sponsor, your only obligation will be going to the mailbox every month to pick up your check.

If you are interested in starting a conversation about being a passive investor, go to Haydencrabtree.com/investor. When you sign up on that page, I will email you some details on what kind of projects I am working on and you will get sent an alert any time I have a deal that you can invest in with me.

CHAPTER 60

YOU HAVE TIME BUT NO MONEY

This is where I started out back in college. I had ample time, but I was a poor college kid who did not have a big bank account. My personal journey led me to finding a mentor and working for him for free for over a year to learn the ropes of real estate investing. Luckily for you, I have just shared a ton of knowledge with you and have shortcutted your journey. (I really wish I had this book when I was first getting started)

You could take the same path that I did and find an investor near you and ask to shadow them. If you can shadow them and see them do a couple of deals, you can then begin to use their experience to build up your track record. Once you have a few deals under your belt, you begin to gain confidence and can have educated conversations with potential investors.

It is extremely important that you realize most active and successful investors will not let you shadow them. This worked successfully for me because I was willing to *give give give!* I would give my time and do the best I possibly could, asking for nothing in return. I was willing to learn and add value to his business without asking for anything.

If I was stingy with my time or lazy and was taking up their valuable free time, the mentor relationship would not have worked as well as it did. If you are going to find a mentor, be sure to find ways to add value to their life and their business first. *When someone successful gives you their time, respect that and treat it like gold.*

The most successful investors do not want to waste their own time on someone who is going to flake out. If you do get a meeting, always respect their time. Be sure to show up early, dress professionally, do your research on them beforehand and ask educated questions. If they deny you a meeting, find a way to add value to them. Find interesting articles that could benefit them and send it to them. Find some deals that you feel like are good and bring them to the investor. Be creative and make it happen!

Another option for you would be to live extremely lean and save as much cash as possible. It will be tough, but if you want it bad enough, you can find a way to save up enough money to buy your first investment.

There are strategies such as getting 0% interest credit cards and pulling the cash out to buy properties. Or "house hacking" your way to your first property. You can even lease and then sublease properties out to begin building cash flow and a nest egg to put into your first deal. With education you can find deals like I did that makes $108k a year with no money down. That case study can be found in the back of this book.

You may be tempted to jump right in and try to go out and raise money. I applaud you for this and I always want you to keep your eyes on that prize. The truth is that you should do a deal with your own money before you do a deal with investors.

You will learn so much on your first deal about how to buy, manage and profit from real estate. I have been told and agree with the idea that even if you do not make any money on your first deal you should still do it. The amount of information you will learn will stick with you for life and you will have an invaluable education. Of course, you should always aim to make money!

CHAPTER 61

YOU HAVE MONEY AND TIME

This could be you if you run an internet business that makes a lot of money, but doesn't require a lot of time. Or maybe you are retired and are looking for something to do so that you can make some money and keep yourself busy. Whatever the case may be, if you have money and time then I would suggest you get started investing in real estate yourself, with your own money.

From the lessons you have learned in this book you will have an amazing head start and a very good path to get started. The amount of cash you have will determine the size of your first investment.

As Warren Buffet says, "Do not test the depths of the river with both feet." I would also suggest that you not spend all your money on your first project. Your first project will teach you many lessons, and some of them may be expensive. Do not let that prohibit you from getting started. All successful investors had a first project that taught them many lessons.

You should continue educating yourself with books, seminars and training. I do not understand why so many people want to dive head first into college for an education that is going to cost $100,000+ but they are not willing to spend any time or money on courses or seminars that cost 1/10th the price and actually teach you how to make money and become a better, more effective human.

I love courses, seminars and coaching. I am constantly learning from others to optimize my life and you should be too.

If you are ready to take action and execute on what you learned, I'd encourage you to apply to my coaching program.

This program has been designed from the ground up to take you from wherever you are now in your real estate journey, and guide you through your first successful real estate deal.

It's not for everyone, and requires an application to be accepted, but for the right person I truly believe it will change your life forever. I'd encourage you to learn more at HaydenCrabtree.com/Academy.

Lastly, you can find links to *every* resource mentioned in this book (along with video training diving deep into each of the topics mentioned here at no extra cost to you) at HaydenCrabtree.com/Resources.

CHAPTER 62

CONCLUSION

Thank you for choosing this book and investing in yourself!

I wrote this book for the person who I talk to every week that wants to live a better life and have more wealth, but doesn't understand in their core how they can make that happen. I hope this book has opened your eyes to the unique powers of real estate that creates so much wealth for those that choose to get involved.

It is with great confidence I tell you that once you correctly invest in real estate, you will be hooked on its benefits forever!

If there is any way I can help you out, please reach out to me and I will help you. You can get a hold of me on instagram @HaydenCrabtree by sending me a direct message or you can submit a question at HaydenCrabtree.com/ resources. It may take me a minute to get back to you as I am running a business during the day.

Snap a picture with the book and tag me in an instagram post and I'll send you a special goodie to help you get started on your real estate journey. This is your journey to financial freedom and living the life of your dreams.

If you found this book valuable, please text or email this link to someone you care about: HaydenCrabtree.com/resources

I will send them a copy of this book for free and they can enjoy the lessons too. From there you two can hold each other accountable, and possibly even partner on deals together.

Please do me that favor and send the link right now if you found any piece of information here useful.

As we wrap up I want to reiterate how important it is that you not only absorb this knowledge, but more importantly use it.

Knowledge without action is useless. You now have the knowledge that very few people in the world do. Use it!

Get out of your comfort zone and take action today!

ABOUT THE AUTHOR

Hi! My name is Hayden Crabtree and I am so glad you have read my book. This book and all the information in it is what I have dedicated my life to since I was 19. I had a passion for business and entrepreneurship, but wasn't learning much in college that would actually help me make money.

At that time, I dove in head first to learn all I could about money, wealth and business. A common thread I kept coming across was that many wealthy people had their hands in real estate. At this point I knew nothing about real estate, but was very anxious to learn.

I sought out a mentor who was a full time real estate investor and worked for him for free for over a year. During this process I learned more than you could ever imagine from college or any book. I got my hands dirty with every aspect of real estate.

After several years of working real estate full time, I realized that not only was I passionate about building wealth in real estate for myself, but I am also passionate about helping others take advantage of the huge benefits of real estate that almost no one knows about!

Today I am an active real estate investor that lives in Atlanta, GA, and invests all over the southeast. Currently I invest in self storage facilities. I help other people who want to invest with me in those deals to earn passive cash flow, enjoy great tax benefits and also make a lot of equity.

CAN YOU HELP?

Thank You For Reading My Book!

I really appreciate all of your feedback, and I love hearing what you have to say.

I need your input to make the next version of this book and my future books better.

Please leave me an honest review on Amazon letting me know what you thought of the book.

Thanks so much!

~ Hayden Crabtree

BONUS SECTION

To learn about my deal that makes $108,000 a year with no money of my own, go here to download the case study!

HaydenCrabtree.com/Resources